HEALTH CARE CRISIS IN AMERICA

HEALTH CARE CRISIS IN AMERICA

JANET B. PRINCE
EDITOR

Novinka Books
New York

Copyright © 2006 by Nova Science Publishers, Inc.

All rights reserved. No part of this book may be reproduced, stored in a retrieval system or transmitted in any form or by any means: electronic, electrostatic, magnetic, tape, mechanical photocopying, recording or otherwise without the written permission of the Publisher.

For permission to use material from this book please contact us:
Telephone 631-231-7269; Fax 631-231-8515
Web Site: http://www.novapublishers.com

NOTICE TO THE READER

The Publisher has taken reasonable care in the preparation of this book, but makes no expressed or implied warranty of any kind and assumes no responsibility for any errors or omissions. No liability is assumed for incidental or consequential damages in connection with or arising out of information contained in this book. The Publisher shall not be liable for any special, consequential, or exemplary damages resulting, in whole or in part, from the readers' use of, or reliance upon, this material.

This publication is designed to provide accurate and authoritative information with regard to the subject matter covered herein. It is sold with the clear understanding that the Publisher is not engaged in rendering legal or any other professional services. If legal or any other expert assistance is required, the services of a competent person should be sought. FROM A DECLARATION OF PARTICIPANTS JOINTLY ADOPTED BY A COMMITTEE OF THE AMERICAN BAR ASSOCIATION AND A COMMITTEE OF PUBLISHERS.

LIBRARY OF CONGRESS CATALOGING-IN-PUBLICATION DATA
Available upon request

ISBN 1-59454-689-4

Published by Nova Science Publishers, Inc. ✢ *New York*

CONTENTS

Preface		vii
Chapter 1	Health Care Spending: Past Trends and Projections *Paulette C. Morgan*	1
Chapter 2	Overview of the Medicare Prescription Drug, Improvement, and Modernization Act of 2003 *Jennifer O'Sullivan, Hinda Chaikind, Sibyl Tilson, Jennifer Boulanger and Paulette Morgan*	11
Chapter 3	Prescription Drug Importation and Internet Sales: A Legal Overview *Jody Feder*	43
Chapter 4	Health Insurance: A Primer *Bernadette Fernandez*	75
Chapter 5	Health Insurance Coverage: Characteristics of the Insured and Uninsured Populations in 2001 *Chris L. Peterson*	101
Index		109

PREFACE

For those with full health care provided by their employers, the day is bright. But they are becoming more and more like rare birds. Besides the almost 50,000,000 without any health insurance who most frequently let their health deteriorate rather than sitting many hours in emergency rooms, employers are moving towards forcing employees to pay a growing percentage of the ever-escalating price tag. This book presents important information on the trends, laws, and practices in an area of vital interest to virtually everyone in the land.

Chapter 1 focuses on trends in personal health care spending, which includes spending on health care goods and services provided to individuals and excludes expenditures for administrative costs, research, and public health activities. Personal health care expenditures have grown considerably over the past 40 years. Between 1960 and 2002 (the most recent year available), personal health care spending increased from $23.4 billion to $1.6 trillion. It is estimated that personal health spending will exceed $2.9 trillion in 2013. Data on health expenditures suggest four important trends. First, during the 1990s, health spending has grown at lower rates than in the past. However, in 2000, 2001, and 2002 health spending grew at higher rates than the previous decade. Second, health care spending as a percent of gross domestic product (GDP) was relatively constant between 1992 and 2000. Health spending as a percent of GDP increased in 2001 and 2002, indicating that health expenditures are growing faster than the overall economy. Third, four types of health services consistently compose the bulk of health care expenditures: hospital care, physician and clinical services, nursing home and home health care, and prescription drugs. Spending on prescription drugs has grown since 1980 and is projected to continue growing during the next decade. Fourth, over the past 40 years, the primary financing of health care has shifted from out-of-pocket payments to payments by private insurance and the federal government.

On December 8, 2003, the President signed the Medicare Prescription Drug, Improvement, and Modernization Act of 2003, P.L. 108-173. On November 22, 2003, the House of Representatives voted 220 to 215 to approve H.R. 1, the Medicare prescription drug and modernization conference agreement as reported in chapter 2. The Senate voted 54 to 44 to approve the conference agreement on November 25. The Act creates a prescription drug benefit for Medicare beneficiaries and establishes a new Medicare Advantage program to replace the current Medicare+Choice program. The prescription drug benefit, which begins in 2006, is voluntary and beneficiaries would pay a monthly premium after enrolling. Until that time, beneficiaries have access to a drug discount card to obtain discounts on their drug purchases. Medicare Advantage establishes payments based on a system of bids and benchmarks. One area of major difference during the conference was the so-called "premium support" provisions of H.R. 1 whereby the original Medicare fee-for-service program would be required to compete against the new Medicare Advantage program. The Act creates a six-year Comparative Cost Adjustment program in which the concept of premium support would be applied in a limited number of Metropolitan Statistical Areas (MSAs). The Act also provides a stabilization fund to create incentives for plans to enter into and remain in the Medicare Advantage program. The Act includes a measure that would require congressional consideration of legislation if general revenue funding for the entire Medicare program exceeds 45%. In addition, beginning in 2007, the Medicare Part B premium will be increased for high-income beneficiaries; it will be phased-in over five years. The Part B deductible increases to $110 in 2005 and will be indexed beginning in 2006. The Act contains numerous provisions that generally increase fee-for-service Medicare payments, especially for rural health care providers, and modify numerous regulatory and administrative practices. The Act also makes changes to the Medicaid program and authorizes new tax-advantaged accounts for medical expenses called health savings accounts. Under Congress's FY2004 budget resolution, $400 billion was reserved for Medicare modernization, creation of a prescription drug benefit, and, in the Senate, to promote geographic equity payment. The Congressional Budget Office (CBO) estimated that the conference agreement for H.R. 1 would increase direct (or mandatory) spending by $394.3 billion from FY2004 through FY2013. Prescription drug spending is estimated at $409.8 billion over the 10-year period and Medicare Advantage spending at $14.2 billion. The fee-for-service provisions are estimated to save $21.5 billion over the 10-year period and the cost containment measures are estimated to save $13.3 billion over the period.

As prescription drug prices have escalated in recent years, so too has consumer interest in purchasing less costly medications abroad. Meanwhile, in July, 2003, the House of Representatives passed H.R. 2427, a bill that would allow wholesalers, pharmacists, and consumers to import certain prescription drugs from 25 different countries, including Canada, where drug prices are often lower than in the United States. Although H.R. 2427 passed the House, the provisions allowing drug importation faced opposition in the Senate and were not included in the conference agreement on Medicare prescription drug benefits. Instead, the final Medicare bill, H.R. 1, modified a provision of existing law that authorizes the Food and Drug Administration (FDA) to allow the importation of prescription drugs if the Secretary of Health and Human Services certifies that implementing such a program is safe and reduces costs, a determination that no Secretary has made in the years since a similar certification requirement was established in 2000. Despite the compromise reached in the final Medicare bill, the debate about drug importation continues. On the one hand, the FDA and some lawmakers remain opposed to allowing prescription drugs to be imported from foreign countries, arguing that the FDA cannot guarantee the safety of such drugs. On the other hand, importation proponents, who claim that importation would result in significantly lower prices for U.S. consumers, say that safety concerns are overblown and would recede if additional precautions were implemented. Just as the FDA has expressed concerns about the safety of imported drugs, federal regulators have become increasingly worried about the risks posed by some online pharmacies and Internet drug sales. Indeed, the regulation of prescription drug importation and the oversight of online pharmacies often overlap because many consumers use online pharmacies to purchase imported drugs. Regardless of whether or not drugs purchased online are imported, the FDA is worried about the safety of such medications because of its concern that a small number of online doctors and pharmacies are exploiting regulatory gaps to prescribe and dispense illegal, addictive, or unsafe drugs. In response to concerns about prescription drug imports and Internet sales, several congressional lawmakers have introduced the following bills: H.R. 616, H.R. 780, H.R. 847, H.R. 2497, H.R. 2652, H.R. 2717, H.R. 2769, S. 1781, S. 1974, and S. 1992. Currently, the following federal and state agencies are involved in regulating aspects of prescription drug importation and Internet sales: the Food and Drug Administration, the U.S. Customs and Border Protection (CBP), the Drug Enforcement Agency (DEA), state boards of pharmacy, and state medical boards. Although chapter 3 is intended to focus on legal aspects of prescription drug importation and Internet sales, both legal and policy issues are addressed because they are closely linked.

People buy insurance to protect themselves against possible financial loss in the future. Such losses may be due to a motor vehicle collision, natural disaster, or other circumstance. For patients, financial losses may result from the use of medical services. Health insurance then provides protection against the possibility of financial loss due to health care use. In addition, since people do not know ahead of time exactly what their health care expenses will be, paying for health insurance on a regular basis helps smooth out their spending. While health insurance continues to be mainly a private enterprise in this country, government plays an increasingly significant role. Especially during the latter half of the 20th century, the government both initiated and responded to dynamics in medicine, the economy, and the workplace through legislation and public policies. For example, the Internal Revenue Service clarified that employer contributions to employee health benefits are exempt from taxation, which encouraged the growth of employment-based health coverage. Given the frequent introduction of legislation aimed at modifying or building on the current health insurance system, understanding the potential impact of such proposals requires a working knowledge of how health insurance is designed, provided, purchased, and regulated. Chapter 4 provides basic information about those topics. Persons and families without health coverage are more likely than those with coverage to forgo needed health care, which often leads to worse health outcomes and the need for expensive medical treatment. Since uninsured persons are more likely to be poor than insured persons, the uninsured are less able to afford the health care they need. Uninsurance can lead to health care access problems for communities, such as overcrowding in emergency rooms. Furthermore, individual states and the nation as a whole are affected through increased taxes and health care prices to cover uncompensated care expenses. Americans obtain health insurance in different settings and through a variety of methods. People may get health coverage through the private sector, or from a publicly funded program. Consumers may purchase health insurance on their own, as part of an employee group, or through a trade or professional association. A small minority of employees get health insurance at no up-front cost because their employer pays the total insurance premium. However, 45 million Americans did not have health coverage for the entire year of 2003. Health insurance benefits are delivered and financed under different systems. The factors that distinguish one delivery system from another are many, including how health care is financed, how much access to providers and services is controlled, and how much authority the enrollee has to design her/his health plan. To illustrate, managed care is characterized by predetermined restrictions on accessing services, whereas individual decision-making regarding use of health benefits is a hallmark of consumer-driven health care. And as economic conditions change, a specific delivery system may gain or lose the interest of affected parties.

The number of Americans without health insurance rose in 2001 to 41.2 million Americans (14.6%) — an increase of 1.4 million people from 2000. This reversed a two-year trend of falling numbers of uninsured. Approximately 1.3 million fewer Americans had employment-based health coverage, compared to 2000, according to the Census Bureau. From 1999 to 2000, this number had risen by 2.9 million. In spite of the decline, most Americans (64.1%) still received their health insurance through an employer. Yet full-time, full-year workers and their family members made up more than half of the uninsured. The percentage of individuals covered by Medicaid increased significantly in 2001. Among children in 2001, the percentage of uninsured did not change significantly. Chapter 5 examines characteristics of both the insured and the uninsured populations in the United States.

In: Health Care Crisis in America
Editor: Janet B. Prince, pp. 1-10

ISBN: 1-59454-689-4
© 2006 Nova Science Publishers, Inc.

Chapter 1

HEALTH CARE SPENDING: PAST TRENDS AND PROJECTIONS[*]

Paulette C. Morgan

SUMMARY

This article focuses on trends in personal health care spending, which includes spending on health care goods and services provided to individuals and excludes expenditures for administrative costs, research, and public health activities. Personal health care expenditures have grown considerably over the past 40 years. Between 1960 and 2002 (the most recent year available), personal health care spending increased from $23.4 billion to $1.6 trillion. It is estimated that personal health spending will exceed $2.9 trillion in 2013.

Data on health expenditures suggest four important trends. First, during the 1990s, health spending has grown at lower rates than in the past. However, in 2000, 2001, and 2002 health spending grew at higher rates than the previous decade. Second, health care spending as a percent of gross domestic product (GDP) was relatively constant between 1992 and 2000. Health spending as a percent of GDP increased in 2001 and 2002, indicating that health expenditures are growing faster than the overall economy. Third, four types of health services consistently compose the bulk of health care expenditures: hospital care, physician and clinical services, nursing home

---
[*] Excerpted from CRS Report for Congress RL31094, Updated April 8, 2004.

and home health care, and prescription drugs. Spending on prescription drugs has grown since 1980 and is projected to continue growing during the next decade. Fourth, over the past 40 years, the primary financing of health care has shifted from out-of-pocket payments to payments by private insurance and the federal government.

GROWTH IN SPENDING

In 2002 (the most recent year available), over $1.6 trillion was spent on health care and health-related activities.[1] **Table 1** indicates how this amount was spent. Data on national health expenditures include spending on a broad range of health-related activities. A small portion of 2002 health expenditures (about $213 billion, or 14%) was spent on administrative costs, net cost of private health insurance,[2] government public health activities, research,[3] and construction. However, the vast majority of 2002 health expenditures was spent on personal health care. Personal health care includes goods and services provided to individuals to treat or prevent medical conditions. The remainder of this article will focus on personal health care expenditures.

Spending on personal health care continues to increase every year. Between 1960 and 2002, expenditures for personal health care grew from $23.4 billion to $1.3 trillion; in 2013, personal health care spending is projected to exceed $2.9 trillion. **Figure 1** tracks past and projected growth rates of personal health care spending in nominal terms (i.e., not adjusted for inflation). From the beginning of 1994 to the end of 1999, health spending increased at an average annual rate of 5.4%. This low growth is attributable to changes in both the private and public sectors. In the private sector, the increased use of managed care limited cost growth during the mid-1990s. Vigorous fraud-and-abuse investigation and the Balanced Budget Act of 1997 (which slowed growth in hospital, home health, and nursing home payments) constrained health expenditures in the late 1990s.[4] The effects of these changes in public and private sector have subsided. Personal health expenditures have increased each year from a 6.6% increase in 2000, and an 8.5% increase in 2001, to an 8.8% increase in 2002 — the highest growth rate since 1991. Yet, looking from a broader historical perspective, spending growth in 2002 was still much lower than that in most years since 1960 (see **Figure 1**). In particular, the years 1979 through 1981 experienced growth rates between 13.8% and 16.1%. Between 2003 and 2013, personal health care spending is projected to increase at an average rate of about 7% per year.

Table 1. 2002 Health Expenditures

Type of Expenditure	Amount ($ billions)	Increase over 2001 spending ($ billions)	Percent increase over 2001 spending
Personal health care expenditures:			
Hospital care	$486.5	$42.2	9.5%
Physician and clinical services	$339.5	$24.4	7.7%
Long-term care:			
Nursing home care	$103.2	$4.1	4.1%
Home health care	$36.1	$2.4	7.2%
Prescription drugs	$162.4	$21.6	15.3%
Dental services	$70.3	$4.7	7.2%
Other professional services	$45.9	$3.2	7.6%
Non-durable medical goods (excluding prescription drugs)	$31.7	$0.7	2.3%
Durable medical goods	$18.8	$0.6	3.3%
Other personal health care	$45.8	$4.9	12.1%
Total personal health care expenditures	**$1,340.2**	**$108.8**	**8.8%**
Government administration and net cost of private health insurance	$105.0	$14.6	16.2%
Government public health activities	$51.2	$2.8	5.9%
Research	$34.3	$2.8	8.9%
Construction	$22.4	$3.2	16.8%
Total national health expenditures	**$1,553.0**	**$132.3**	**9.3%**

Source: Prepared by the Congressional Research Service (CRS) based on data from the Centers for Medicare and Medicaid Services, Office of the Actuary.

A combination of factors can cause nominal spending to increase: rising prices, population growth, increases in the quantity of medical services each person receives, advances in medical knowledge and technology, and other factors. Expenditures attributable to non-price factors are often referred to as "real" spending. Growth in real spending represents a quantitative and qualitative increase in the level of medical care that individuals are receiving and can indicate an improvement in the population's standard of living.[5] Conversely, increases in health care expenditures attributable to higher prices represent only a pecuniary transfer from the payer to the providers and manufacturers of medical goods and services. **Figure 2** depicts the share of nominal spending growth attributable to increases in medical care prices, increases in population, and increases in per capita real health expenditures (what some experts describe as the "intensity" of care). For much of the time period shown in **Figure 2**, prices played a larger role in nominal spending increases than population or non-price factors (e.g., improved medical technology or higher utilization). During the late 1990s, medical care prices, constrained by managed care, grew at lower rates than in any other year shown. Price growth is projected to increase during the next decade, though not to the high levels experienced during the 1970s and 1980s.

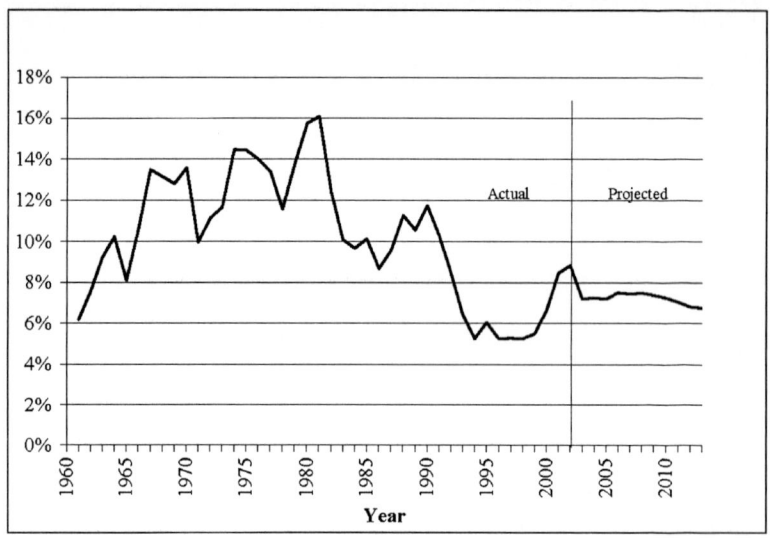

Source: CRS calculations using data from the Centers for Medicare and Medicaid Services, Office of the Actuary.

Figure 1. Growth in Nominal Personal Health Care Expenditures

However, currently available price indexes may not accurately reflect changes in medical care prices. Ideally, a price index would measure only how much must be paid this year to receive the same level of care as that received in some base period, holding quality constant. But it is difficult to hold the quality of care constant over time considering the rate of medical advances. For example, heart surgeries today are of higher quality than those performed in the past, as measured by survival rates. Yet, price indices tend to treat both procedures as equal in quality. Thus, measures of increases in the price of heart surgeries capture both pure price increases as well as quality increases, which violates the basic principle of price indexes. By including quality effects in price measures, price indexes tend to overstate true increases in medical prices.[6]

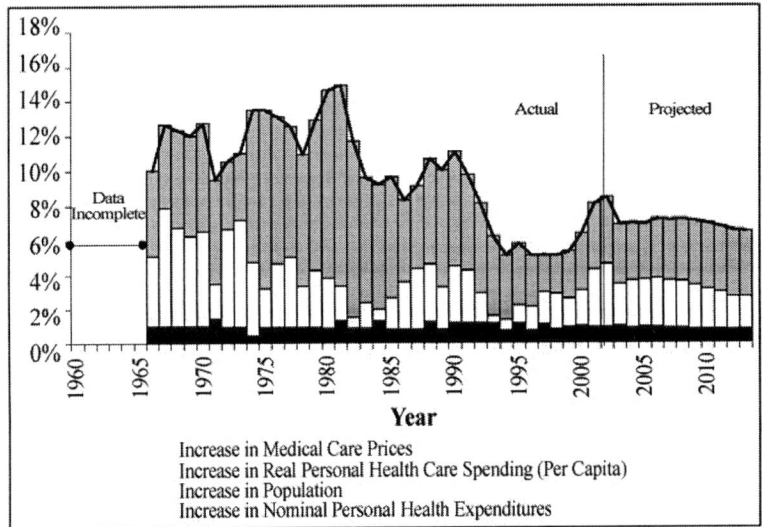

Source: CRS calculations using data from the U.S. Census Bureau and the Centers for Medicare and Medicaid Services, Office of the Actuary.

Note: To make component factors additive, percentages in this figure represent continuous growth rates rather than discrete annual changes. Continuous growth rates can be converted to discrete yearly changes using the formula: [(annual change)=exp(continuous rate)-1].

Figure 2. Factors Influencing Growth in Nominal Personal Health Expenditures

HEALTH SPENDING AND GROSS DOMESTIC PRODUCT

Personal health expenditures as a percent of GDP have risen since 1960. This trend has two implications: (1) personal health care spending is growing faster than the overall economy, and (2) a larger share of the nation's economic resources is being devoted to providing medical goods and services to the population. **Figure 3** depicts past and projected personal health care spending as a percent of GDP. In 1960, personal health care expenditures were about 4% of GDP; in 2002, they were 13%. Much of this growth occurred between 1960 and 1991. Between 1992 and 2000, personal health expenditures as a percent of GDP remained between 11.5% and

11.7%. This relative constancy indicates that expenditures were growing at about the same rate as the overall economy. In 2001, however, personal health care expenditures grew to 12.3% of GDP, an indication that personal health care spending grew faster than the overall economy in that year. It is projected that personal health care spending will continue to grow faster than the overall economy, accounting for almost 16% of GDP in 2013.

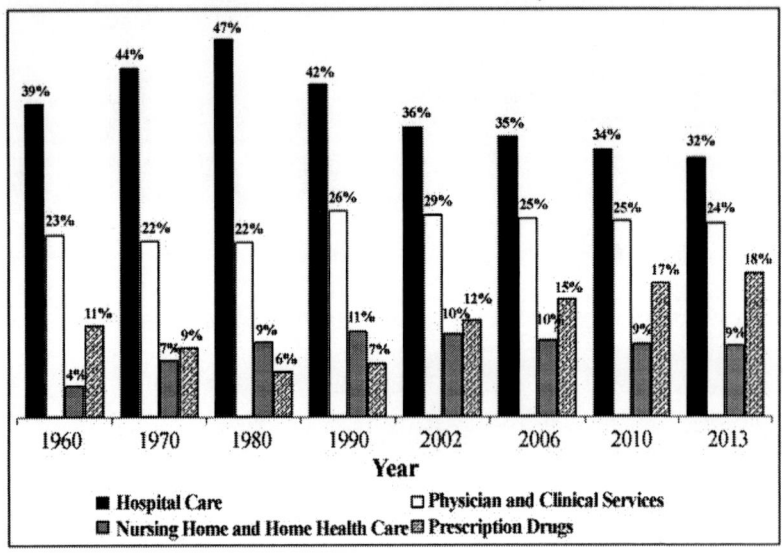

Source: CRS calculations using data from the Centers for Medicare and Medicaid Services, Office of the Actuary.

Figure 3. Personal Health Care Spending as a Percent of Gross Domestic Product (GDP)

SPENDING ON SPECIFIC CATEGORIES OF HEALTH CARE

Of the total amount spent on personal health care, the largest categories of expenditures tend to be hospital care, physician and clinical services, nursing home and home health care, and prescription drugs. The contribution of these four categories to personal health spending has remained fairly constant, averaging 84% of total personal health care spending over the last four decades. However, the relative sizes of these categories have changed over time. **Figure 4** depicts past and projected spending on each of these categories as a percent of personal health care spending. Expenditures on hospital care, as a percent of personal health spending, have decreased from 47% in 1980 to 36% in 2002. They are projected to decrease further in the future. This trend indicates that spending on hospital care is growing at a slower rate than spending on other categories of personal health care. Spending on prescription drugs as a percent of personal health care spending has increased from 6% in 1980 to 12% in 2002. It is projected to continue increasing through the next decade. Such a trend indicates that spending on prescription drugs is rising faster than other categories of personal health care. **Figure 4** probably underestimates the impact of prescription drugs on personal health care expenditures. Data on drug spending reflect prescription drugs obtained from retail pharmacies, but it excludes drugs provided by institutional pharmacies. Drugs dispensed to patients from a hospital or nursing home pharmacy are excluded from the prescription drug category. Instead, spending on drugs dispensed from institutional pharmacies is implicit in the amount spent for services at the respective institutions (e.g., hospital services or nursing home care).

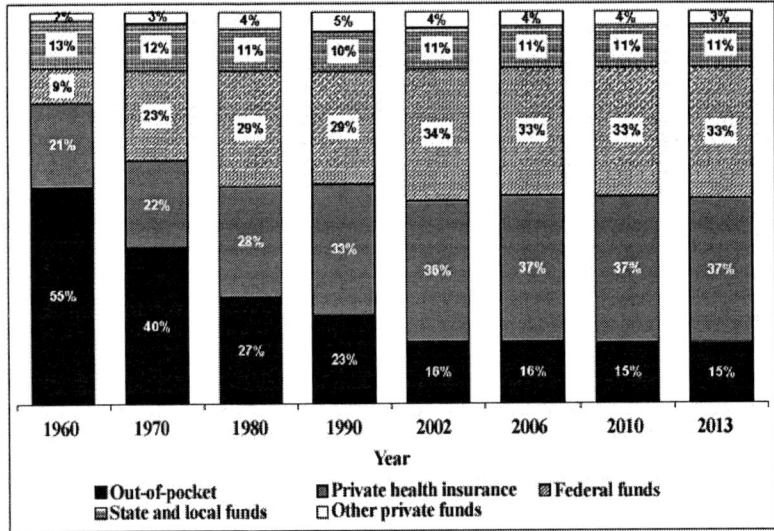

Source: CRS calculations using data from the Centers for Medicare and Medicaid Services, Office of the Actuary.

Figure 4. Major Categories of Personal Health Care Spending as a Percent of Total Personal health Expenditures

WHO PAYS FOR HEALTH CARE?

Direct payments for personal health care come from five general sources: consumer payments out-of-pocket, payments by private insurance companies, federal funds, state and local funds, and "other" private funds. Out-of-pocket payments include payments by those without health insurance. Out-of-pocket payments also include payments by the insured for deductibles, coinsurance, and costs not covered by insurance (excluding premiums). "Other" private funds consist mostly of philanthropic contributions to the health care system.

Ultimately, all health care spending is paid for by individuals through direct payments, cost-sharing, insurance premiums,[7] taxes, and charitable contributions. However, most of these payments are redistributed; what a person pays does not necessarily reflect how much health care that person receives. One who pays relatively high taxes might not have any of their health care financed by the government. Similarly, there are some people who pay health insurance premiums, yet use less care than the sum of the premiums paid. Only when individuals pay directly for the cost of treatment (either because they are uninsured or because they have not met their deductible) do personal expenditures directly reflect the amount of care received.

Figure 5 shows the percent of personal health care spending attributable to each source. In 1960, 55% of all personal health care was financed out-of-pocket, whereas private insurance paid for 21% and the federal government paid for 9%. In 2002, only 16% of personal health care was paid out-of-pocket while private insurance paid for 36% and the federal government paid for 34%. Much of the increase in the federal government's share of health spending occurred during the 1960s, when the Medicare and Medicaid programs were introduced. The increase in the federal government's share of payments during the 1990s is likely due to the ability of private insurance to reduce its share of expenditures through managed care. Furthermore, during this period, there was a dramatic increase in the quality and cost of health services.

Health Care Spending: Past Trends and Projections

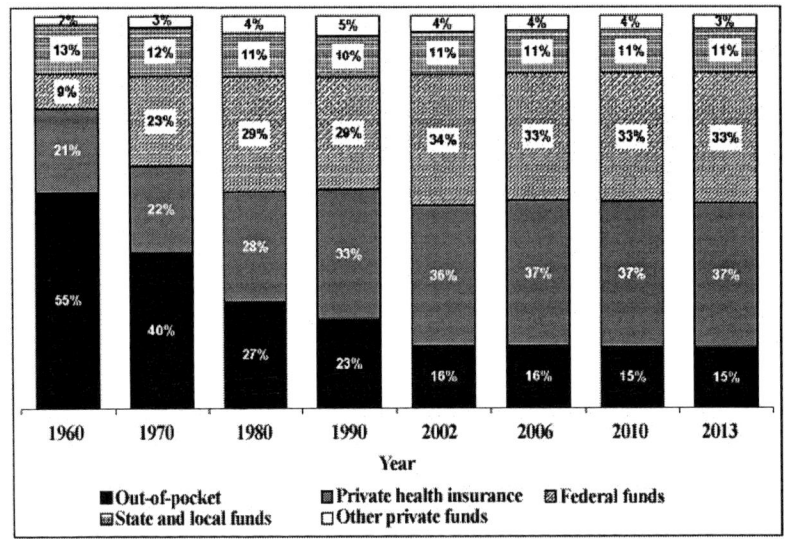

Source: CRS calculations using data from the Centers for Medicare and Medicaid Services, Office of the Actuary.

Figure 5. Source of Payment for Personal Health Care as a Percent of Total Personal Health Care Expenditures

REFERENCES

[1] All dollar figures cited in this report were obtained from the Centers for Medicare and Medicaid Services (CMS), Office of the Actuary. All percentages were calculated by Congressional Research Service (CRS) using data from CMS.

[2] Net cost of private health insurance is equal to the difference between all premiums paid to insurance providers minus what insurance providers must pay for the provision of health care to its members.

[3] Research excludes amounts spent by pharmaceutical manufacturers, medical equipment suppliers, and other companies. Expenditures on research and development by such entities are implicitly included in the spending figures for other categories, e.g., prescription drugs and durable medical equipment.

[4] Levit, Katharine, Cynthia Smith, Cathy Cowan, Helen Lazenby, and Anne Martin, *Inflation Spurs Spending in 2000. Health Affairs.* v. 21, no. 1, January/February 2002.

[5] In general, higher consumption of goods and services (medical and non-medical alike) is usually viewed as improving the standard of living for an individual. However, some experts might argue that higher utilization is not always indicative of a higher standard of living. For example, an outbreak of a contagious disease would increase the utilization of health services, yet no one would claim that those infected would have a higher standard of living.

[6] For more information, see Berndt, Ernst R., David M. Cutler, Richard G. Frank, Zvi Griliches, Joseph P. Newhouse, and Jack E. Triplett. "Price Indexes for Medical Care Goods and Services: An Overview of Measurement Issues." Published in *Medical Care Output and Productivity*, edited by David M. Cutler and Ernst R. Berndt. (Chicago: The University of Chicago Press, 2001)

[7] Even if the employer is contributing all or a portion of the insurance premium, individual workers generally accept lower wages in exchange for this benefit. Thus, they pay for employer contributions to health care in the form of reduced wages that are lower than what they would otherwise be paid if the employer offered no health benefits.

In: Health Care Crisis in America
Editor: Janet B. Prince, pp. 11-43

ISBN: 1-59454-689-4
© 2006 Nova Science Publishers, Inc.

Chapter 2

OVERVIEW OF THE MEDICARE PRESCRIPTION DRUG, IMPROVEMENT, AND MODERNIZATION ACT OF 2003[*]

Jennifer O'Sullivan, Hinda Chaikind, Sibyl Tilson, Jennifer Boulanger and Paulette Morgan

SUMMARY

On December 8, 2003, the President signed the Medicare Prescription Drug, Improvement, and Modernization Act of 2003, P.L. 108-173. On November 22, 2003, the House of Representatives voted 220 to 215 to approve H.R. 1, the Medicare prescription drug and modernization conference agreement. The Senate voted 54 to 44 to approve the conference agreement on November 25.

The Act creates a prescription drug benefit for Medicare beneficiaries and establishes a new Medicare Advantage program to replace the current Medicare+Choice program. The prescription drug benefit, which begins in 2006, is voluntary and beneficiaries would pay a monthly premium after enrolling. Until that time, beneficiaries have access to a drug discount card to obtain discounts on their drug purchases.

---

[*] Excerpted from CRS Report for Congress RL31966, Updated December 6, 2004.

Medicare Advantage establishes payments based on a system of bids and benchmarks. One area of major difference during the conference was the so-called "premium support" provisions of H.R. 1 whereby the original Medicare fee-for-service program would be required to compete against the new Medicare Advantage program. The Act creates a six-year Comparative Cost Adjustment program in which the concept of premium support would be applied in a limited number of Metropolitan Statistical Areas (MSAs). The Act also provides a stabilization fund to create incentives for plans to enter into and remain in the Medicare Advantage program.

The Act includes a measure that would require congressional consideration of legislation if general revenue funding for the entire Medicare program exceeds 45%. In addition, beginning in 2007, the Medicare Part B premium will be increased for high-income beneficiaries; it will be phased-in over five years. The Part B deductible increases to $110 in 2005 and will be indexed beginning in 2006. The Act contains numerous provisions that generally increase fee-for-service Medicare payments, especially for rural health care providers, and modify numerous regulatory and administrative practices. The Act also makes changes to the Medicaid program and authorizes new tax-advantaged accounts for medical expenses called health savings accounts.

Under Congress's FY2004 budget resolution, $400 billion was reserved for Medicare modernization, creation of a prescription drug benefit, and, in the Senate, to promote geographic equity payment. The Congressional Budget Office (CBO) estimated that the conference agreement for H.R. 1 would increase direct (or mandatory) spending by $394.3 billion from FY2004 through FY2013. Prescription drug spending is estimated at $409.8 billion over the 10-year period and Medicare Advantage spending at $14.2 billion. The fee-for-service provisions are estimated to save $21.5 billion over the 10-year period and the cost containment measures are estimated to save $13.3 billion over the period.

OVERVIEW

On December 8, 2003, the President signed the Medicare Prescription Drug, Improvement, and Modernization Act of 2003. Earlier, the House of Representatives voted 220 to 215 to approve H.R. 1, the conference agreement, on November 22, 2003. The Senate voted 54 to 44 to approve the conference agreement on November 25.

The Act adds a prescription drug benefit and replaces the existing Medicare+Choice program with a new program, called the Medicare Advantage program. The prescription drug benefit, which begins in 2006, is voluntary and beneficiaries would pay a monthly premium after enrolling. Until that time, beneficiaries have access to a drug discount card to obtain discounts on their drug purchases.

Medicare Advantage establishes payments based on a system of bids and benchmarks. One area of major difference during the conference was the so-called "premium support" provisions of H.R. 1 whereby the original Medicare fee-for-service program would be required to compete against the new Medicare Advantage program. The Act creates a six-year Comparative Cost Adjustment program in which the concept of premium support would be applied in a limited number of Metropolitan Statistical areas (MSAs). The Act also provides a stabilization fund to create incentive for plans to enter into and remain in the Medicare Advantage program.

The Act includes a measure that would require congressional consideration of legislation if general revenue funding for the entire Medicare program exceeds 45%. In addition, beginning in 2007, the Medicare Part B premium will be increased for high-income beneficiaries; it will be phased-in over five years. The Part B deductible increases to $110 in 2005 and will be indexed beginning in 2006. The Act contains numerous provisions that generally increase fee-for-service Medicare payments, especially for rural health care providers, and modify numerous regulatory and administrative practices.

Under Congress's FY2004 budget resolution, $400 billion was reserved for Medicare modernization, creation of a prescription drug benefit, and, in the Senate, to promote geographic equity payment, under Congress' FY2004 budget resolution. The Congressional Budget Office (CBO) estimated that the conference agreement for H.R. 1 would increase direct (or mandatory) spending by $394.3 billion from FY2004 through FY2013. Prescription drug spending is estimated at $409.8 billion over the 10-year period and Medicare Advantage spending at $14.2 billion. The fee-for-service provisions are estimated to save $21.5 billion over the 10-year period and the cost containment measures are estimated to save $13.3 billion over the period.[1]

PRESCRIPTION DRUGS

Voluntary Prescription Drug Benefit Program

Overview

The legislation establishes a new Voluntary Prescription Drug Benefit Program under a new Part D of Title XVIII of the Social Security Act. Effective January 1, 2006, a new optional benefit will be established under a new Part D. Beneficiaries will be able to purchase either "standard coverage" or alternative coverage with actuarially equivalent benefits. In 2006, "standard coverage" will have a $250 deductible, 25% coinsurance for costs between $251 and $2,250, then no coverage until the beneficiary has out-of-pocket costs of $3,600 ($5,100 in total spending). Once the beneficiary reaches the catastrophic limit, the program will pay all costs except for nominal cost-sharing. Low-income subsidies will be provided for persons with incomes below 150% of poverty. Coverage will be provided through prescription drug plans or Medicare Advantage prescription drug (MA-PD) plans. The program will rely on private plans to provide coverage and to bear some of the financial risk for drug costs; federal subsidies covering the bulk of the risk will be provided to encourage participation. Plans will determine payments and will be expected to negotiate prices.

Eligibility and Enrollment

Each individual entitled to Medicare Part A or enrolled in Medicare Part B will be entitled to obtain qualified prescription drug coverage through enrollment in a prescription drug plan. A beneficiary enrolled in a Medicare Advantage (MA) plan (see below) providing qualified prescription drug coverage (MA-PD plan) will obtain coverage through that plan. In general, MA enrollees may not enroll in a prescription drug plan under Part D.

The Secretary is required to establish a process for enrollment, disenrollment, termination, and change of enrollment of eligible beneficiaries in prescription drug plans. The Secretary is required to use rules similar to, and coordinated with rules established for MA-PD plans. A six-month initial enrollment period, beginning November 15, 2005, will be established for all persons who are eligible beneficiaries on that date; it is the same period established for enrollment for MA plans for that year. An initial enrollment period will apply for individuals becoming eligible after that date; in no case can such period be less than six months.

The Secretary is required to conduct activities that are designed to broadly disseminate information to eligible beneficiaries and prospective eligible beneficiaries. It must be available at least 30 days prior to the initial enrollment period. The information dissemination requirements are similar to and are to be coordinated with the activities the Secretary is required to perform for MA plans. Comparative information is to include information on benefits and formularies under a plan; monthly beneficiary premium; and beneficiary cost-sharing.

Prescription Drug Benefits

The legislation specifies the requirements for qualified prescription drug coverage. Qualified coverage is defined as either "standard prescription drug coverage" or "alternative prescription drug coverage" with at least actuarially equivalent benefits. In both cases, access would have to be provided to negotiated prices for covered drugs. Plans are permitted to provide supplemental prescription coverage consisting of either certain reductions in cost-sharing (i.e., reduction in deductible, reduction in coinsurance percentage, and increase in initial coverage limit) or coverage of drugs which are excluded because of application of the Medicaid definition of covered drugs. A PDP sponsor may not offer a plan that provides supplemental benefits unless it also offers a basic plan in the area.

For 2006, "standard prescription drug coverage" is defined as having a $250 deductible; 25% coinsurance up to the initial coverage limit ($2,250, accounting for $750 in total out-of-pocket costs and $2,250 in total spending); then no coverage until the beneficiary had out-of-pocket costs of $3,600 ($5,100 total spending). Once the beneficiary reached the catastrophic ("stop loss") limit, the program would pay costs, except for nominal cost-sharing. The cost-sharing is equal to the greater of: (1) a copayment of $2 for a generic drug or preferred multiple source and $5 for any other drug; or (2) 5% coinsurance. Nothing is to be construed as preventing a PDP sponsor or MA organization from reducing the cost-sharing for preferred or generic drugs. Beginning in 2007, the annual dollar amounts would be increased by the annual percentage increase in average per capita aggregate expenditures for covered outpatient drugs for Medicare beneficiaries for the 12-month period ending in July of the previous year.

Plans will be permitted to substitute cost-sharing requirements, for costs up to the initial coverage limit, that were actuarially consistent with an average expected 25% coinsurance for costs up to the initial coverage limit. They may also apply tiered copayments (i.e., different levels, depending on whether a generic, preferred multiple source, or other drug is used) provided such copayments were actuarially consistent with the average 25% cost-sharing requirements.

The Act specifies incurred costs that count toward meeting the catastrophic limit. Costs are only considered incurred if they are incurred for the deductible, cost-sharing, or benefits not paid because of application of the initial coverage limit. Incurred costs do not include amounts for which no benefits are provided because of the application of a formulary. Costs can be treated as incurred costs only if they were paid by the individual (or by another family member on behalf of the individual), paid on behalf of a low-income individual under the subsidy provisions, or under a state pharmaceutical assistance program. Any costs for which the individual was reimbursed by insurance or otherwise will not count toward incurred costs.

Coverage offered by a PDP plan sponsor or a MA-PD entity will be required to provide beneficiaries with access to negotiated prices. Access must be provided even when no benefits were payable because of the application of cost-sharing or an initial coverage limits. Negotiated prices are to take into account negotiated price concessions, such as discounts, direct or indirect subsidies, rebates, and direct or indirect remunerations, for covered Part D drugs, and include dispensing fees. The PDP sponsor or MA-PD entity is required to disclose to the Secretary the aggregate negotiated price concessions made available to the sponsor or organization and passed through in the form of lower subsidies, lower monthly beneficiary premiums, and lower prices through pharmacies and other dispensers. Manufacturers will be required to disclose pricing information to the Secretary.

Beneficiary Protections for Qualified Prescription Drug Coverage

The Act establishes beneficiary protection requirements for qualified prescription drug plans. PDP plan sponsors are required to disclose to each enrolling beneficiary information about the plan's benefit structure. Sponsors will be required to furnish to enrollees a detailed explanation of benefits when drug benefits were provided, including information on benefits compared to the initial coverage limit and the applicable out-of-pocket threshold.

PDP sponsors are required to permit the participation of any pharmacy that meets the plan's terms and conditions. A PDP could reduce copayments for its enrolled beneficiaries below the otherwise applicable level for drugs dispensed through in-network pharmacies; in no case could the reduction result in an increase in subsidy payments made by the Secretary to the plan. The PDP sponsor is required to secure participation in its network of a sufficient number of pharmacies that dispense drugs directly to patients (other than by mail order) to assure convenient access. The Secretary will establish convenient access rules that are no less favorable to enrollees than rules for convenient access established for the TRICARE Retail Pharmacy program. The rules are to include adequate emergency assess for enrolled beneficiaries. Sponsors will permit enrollees to receive benefits (which may include a 90-day supply) through a community pharmacy, rather than through mail-order, with any differential in charge paid by enrollees.

If a PDP sponsor uses a formulary, it will have to meet certain requirements. A pharmaceutical and therapeutic committee must develop and review the formulary. The committee will be required, when developing and reviewing the formulary, to base clinical decisions on the strength of scientific evidence and standards of practice. The committee must also take into account whether including a particular covered drug in the formulary (or in a particular tier in a formulary) had therapeutic advantages in terms of safety and efficacy. The formulary must include drugs within each therapeutic category and class of covered Part D drugs, although not necessarily all drugs within such categories or classes.

The Secretary is required to request the United States Pharmacopeia to develop in consultation with pharmaceutical benefit managers and other interested parties, a list of categories and classes that may be used by plans. The Secretary's request must also include the revision of such classification from time to time to reflect changes in therapeutic uses of covered drugs and the addition of new covered drugs. The plan sponsor can not change therapeutic categories and classes in a formulary other than at the beginning of a plan year, except as the Secretary may permit to take into account new therapeutic uses and newly approved covered drugs. Each sponsor is required to establish policies and procedures to educate and inform health care providers and enrollees concerning the formulary. Any removal of a drug from the formulary, and any change in the preferred or tier cost-sharing status of a drug, could not occur until appropriate notice had been provided to the Secretary, beneficiaries, and physicians, pharmacies, and pharmacists. The plan must provide for periodic evaluation and analysis of treatment protocols and procedures.

The PDP sponsor will be required to have (directly, or indirectly through arrangements) a cost-effective drug utilization management program; quality assurance measures, a medication therapy management program; and a program to control fraud, waste, and abuse.

Each PDP sponsor will be required to have meaningful procedures for the hearing and resolving of any grievances between the sponsor (including any entity or individual through which the sponsor provided covered benefits) and enrollees. Enrollees will be afforded access to expedited determinations and reconsiderations, in the same manner afforded under

MA. A beneficiary in a plan that provides for tiered cost-sharing can request coverage of a non-preferred drug on the same conditions applicable to preferred drugs, if the prescribing physician determines that the preferred drug for the treatment of the same condition is not as effective for the enrollee or has adverse effects for the enrollee. A PDP will be required to have an exceptions process consistent with guidelines established by the Secretary.

In general, PDP plan sponsors will be required to meet the requirements for independent review and appeals of coverage denials and tiered cost-sharing in the same manner that such requirements applied to MA organizations for fee-for-service benefits. An individual enrolled in a PDP plan may appeal to obtain coverage for a drug not on the formulary only if the prescribing physician determines that all covered Part D drugs on any tier of the formulary for treatment of the same condition would not be as effective for the individual or would have adverse effects for the individual or both. The PDP sponsor will be required to meet requirements related to confidentiality and accuracy of enrollee records in the same manner that such requirements applied to MA organizations.

Each PDP sponsor will provide that each pharmacy that dispenses a covered drug shall inform enrolled beneficiaries at the time of purchase (or at the time of delivery in the case of mail order drugs) of any price differential between the price to the enrollee and the price of the lowest cost generic drug covered under the plan that is therapeutically equivalent and bioequivalent and available at the pharmacy. The Secretary is permitted to waive this requirement.

PDP sponsors are required to issue (and reissue as appropriate) a card or other technology that could be used by an enrolled beneficiary to assure access to negotiated prices for drugs. The Secretary will provide for the development, adoption, or recognition of standards relating to a standardized format for the card or other technology.

Electronic Prescription Program

The Act requires the Secretary to develop electronic prescription standards. The standards apply to prescriptions for covered Part D drugs and required information that are transmitted electronically under an electronic prescription drug program that meets the following requirements. The program must provide for the electronic transmittal of information on eligibility and benefits (including formulary drugs, any tiered formulary structure, and prior authorization requirements), information on the drug being prescribed and other drugs listed in the patient's medication history (including drug-drug interactions), and information on the availability of lower-cost, therapeutically appropriate alternative drugs. Additionally, the program must provide for the electronic transmittal of the patient's medical history. Disclosure of information must meet the requirements of the HIPAA privacy rule and, to the extent feasible, be on an interactive, real-time basis.

Access to a Choice of Qualified Prescription Drug Coverage

The Secretary is required to assure that each beneficiary has available a choice of enrollment in at least 2 qualifying plans in the area in which the beneficiary resides. At least one plan has to be a prescription drug plan. The requirement is not satisfied for an area if only one PDP sponsor or one MA organization offering a MA-PD plan offers all the qualifying plans for the area.

The Act permits the Secretary, in order to assure access, to approve limited risk contracts (as discussed below). Only if access is still not provided, will the Secretary provide for the offering of a fallback plan.

PDP Regions

The Act provides for the establishment of PDP regions. The service area for a plan includes an entire PDP region. The Secretary shall establish, and may revise PDP regions in a manner that is consistent with the requirements for establishment and revision of MA regions. To the extent practicable, PDP regions shall be the same as MA regions. The Secretary may establish different regions if the Secretary determines that it would improve access to drug benefits. A plan can be offered in more than one PDP region, including all PDP regions.

Submission of Bids

Each PDP sponsor is required to submit to the Secretary specified information at the same time and in a similar manner as such information is submitted by MA organizations. The information to be submitted is: (1) information on the prescription drug coverage to be provided; (2) the actuarial value of the qualified prescription drug coverage in the region for a beneficiary with a national average risk profile; (3) information on the bid including the basis for the actuarial value, the portion of the bid attributable to basic coverage and if applicable, the portion attributable to supplemental benefits, and assumptions regarding reinsurance subsidy payments; (4) service area; (5) level of risk assumed including whether the sponsor requires a modification of risk level and if so the extent of the modification; and (6) such other information required by the Secretary..

Plan Approval

The Secretary will review the submitted information for purposes of conducting negotiations with the plan. The Secretary has the authority to negotiate the terms and conditions of the plans. The authority is similar to the authority the Director of the Office of Personnel Management has with respect to Federal Employee Health Benefits (FEHB) plans. The Secretary may not interfere with the negotiations between drug manufacturers and pharmacies and PDP sponsors. Further, the Secretary may not require a particular formulary or institute a price structure for the reimbursement of covered Part D drugs.

After review and negotiation, the Secretary will approve or disapprove the plan. The Secretary may only approve a plan if certain requirements are met. The plan must comply with Part D requirements, including those relating to beneficiary protections. The Secretary must determine that the plan and the sponsor meet requirements relating to actuarial determinations. Further, the Secretary may not find that the design of the plan and its benefits (including any formulary and tiered formulary structure) are likely to discourage enrollment by certain beneficiaries. The Secretary may not make a finding with respect to design of categories and classes within a formulary if such categories and classes are consistent with guidelines (if any) for such categories and classes established by the United States Pharmacopeia.

The Act provides that the Secretary may only approve a limited risk plan for a PDP region if the access requirements for the region would otherwise not be met except for the approval of a limited risk or fallback plan. Only the minimum number of limited risk plans necessary for a region to meet access requirements may be approved. The Secretary shall provide priority to those with the highest level of risk. In no case can the reduction of risk provide for no (or a de minimis) level of financial risk. There is no limit on the number of full risk plans that may be approved.

Fallback

If required access is not provided, including through a limited risk plan, the Act establishes a fallback process. The Secretary is required to establish a separate process for the solicitation of bids from eligible fallback entities. A single fallback entity may not offer all fallback plans throughout the United States. The Secretary can only approve one fallback plan for all fallback service areas in any PDP region for a contract period. Competitive contracting provisions apply. The Secretary shall approve fallback plans so that if there are any fallback service areas in the region for the year, they are offered at the same time as prescription drug plans would otherwise be offered. Fallback prescription drug plans are permitted to offer only standard prescription drug coverage and meet such other requirements specified by the Secretary. The fallback plan would not be permitted to engage in any marketing or branding of the contract.

Under a fallback contract, the Secretary would pay actual costs of Part D covered drugs taking into account negotiated price concessions. Payment would also be made for prescription management fees tied to performance management requirements established by the Secretary. Beneficiary premiums under fallback plans would be uniform and equal to 26% of the Secretary's estimate of the average monthly per capita actuarial cost (including administrative costs) to the entity offering the fallback plan. The federal government would pay the remainder.

In general, contract requirements for fallback plans would be the same as those established for prescription drug plans. A contract for a fallback plan would be for three years (and be renewable after a subsequent bidding process. However, a contract could not apply in an area in any year unless the area was a fallback service area.

Contract Requirements

The Act establishes organizational requirements for PDP sponsors. In general, a PDP sponsor must be licensed under state law as a risk bearing entity eligible to offer health insurance or health benefits coverage in each state in which it offers a prescription drug plan. Alternatively it could meet solvency standards established by the Secretary for entities not licensed by the state. To the extent an entity is at risk, it must assume financial risk on a prospective basis for covered benefits that are not covered by direct subsidy payments. PDP plan sponsors would be required to enter into a contract with the Secretary under which the sponsor agreed to comply both with the applicable requirements and standards and the terms and conditions of payment.

Premiums

The conferees have stated that the average monthly beneficiary premium in 2006 will be $35 and represent, on average, 26% of the cost of the benefit provided. The Act specifies the calculation as follows. The monthly beneficiary premium for a prescription drug plan is defined as the base beneficiary premium, as adjusted. The base beneficiary premium equals the product of the beneficiary premium percentage and the national average monthly bid amount. The beneficiary premium percentage is equal to: (1)

26%, divided by (2)100% minus a percentage equal to total reinsurance payments divided by the sum of such reinsurance payments and total payments the Secretary estimates will be paid to prescription drug plans in a year that are attributable to the standardized bid amount (taking into account amounts paid by the Secretary and enrollees and the application of risk adjustment). The national average monthly bid amount is a weighted average of standardized bid amounts for each prescription drug plan and each MA-PD plan. Once the base beneficiary premium is calculated, it is adjusted up or down, as appropriate, to reflect differences between it and the geographically-adjusted national average monthly bid amount. It is further increased for any supplemental benefits and decreased if the individual is entitled to a low-income subsidy. The premium is uniform for all persons enrolled in the plan, except for those receiving low-income subsidies or those subject to a late enrollment penalty.

Late enrollment penalties would be applied to beneficiaries who failed to maintain creditable coverage for a period of 63 days (within a continuous period of eligibility), beginning on the day after the individual's initial enrollment period and ending on the date of enrollment in a prescription drug plan or MA-PD plan.

Beneficiary premium payments may be paid directly to the PDP sponsor or MA organization. Alternatively the beneficiary has the option of having the amount withheld from his or her social security payment or having payment made through an electronic funds transfer mechanism. Payments withheld are to be paid to the PDP sponsor.

Premium and Cost-Sharing Subsidies for Low-Income Individuals

The Act provides premium and cost-sharing subsidies for low-income subsidy-eligible individuals. There are two groups of subsidy eligible individuals. The first group is composed of persons who: (1) are enrolled in a prescription drug plan or MA-PD plan; (2) have incomes below 135% of poverty; and (3) have resources in 2006 below $6,000 for an individual and $9,000 for a couple (increased in future years by the percentage increase in the CPI). Also included in this group are persons who are dually eligible for Medicare and Medicaid, regardless of whether or not they meet the other eligibility requirements. The second group of subsidy eligible individuals are persons meeting the same requirements, except that the income level is 150% of poverty and an alternative resources standard may be used; this alternative standard in 2006 is $10,000 for an individual and $20,000 for a couple (increased in future years by the percentage increase in the CPI).

Individuals with incomes below 135% of poverty, and resources meeting the requirement for the first group, will have a premium subsidy equal to 100% of the low-income benchmark premium amount (essentially a weighted average for the region), but in no case higher than the actual premium amount for basic coverage under the plan. Other low-income subsidy eligible persons will have a sliding scale premium subsidy ranging from 100% of such value at 135% of poverty to 0% of such value at 150% of poverty. Persons below 135% of poverty will have a premium subsidy for any late enrollment penalty equal to 80% for the first 60 months of delayed enrollment and 100% thereafter.

Beneficiaries in both groups are entitled to cost-sharing subsidies. Individuals with incomes below 135% of poverty, and resources meeting the requirement for the first group will have no deductible, cost-sharing for all costs up to the out-of-pocket threshold of $2 for a generic drug or preferred multiple source and $5 for any other drug. Institutionalized dual eligibles will have no cost-sharing. Full benefit dual eligibles with incomes up to 100% of poverty will have cost-sharing for all costs up to the out-of-pocket threshold of $1 for a generic drug or preferred multiple source and $3 for any other drug. Other low-income subsidy eligible persons will have a $50 deductible, 15% cost-sharing for all costs up to the out-of-pocket limit, and cost-sharing for costs above the out-of-pocket threshold of $2 for a generic drug or preferred multiple source and $5 for any other drug. The deductible amounts are increased each year beginning in 2007 by the annual percentage increase in per capita beneficiary expenditures for Part D covered drugs. The cost-sharing amounts are increased by the increase in the consumer price index.

Eligibility determinations are to be made under the state Medicaid plan for the state or by the Commissioner of Social Security. The determinations shall remain effective for a period determined by the Secretary, not to exceed one year. Full dual eligible persons are to be treated as subsidy eligible persons; the Secretary may provide that other Medicaid beneficiaries be treated as subsidy eligible. The Secretary will provide a process whereby the Secretary will notify the PDP sponsor or MA organization that an individual is eligible for a subsidy and the amount of the subsidy. The sponsor or entity would reduce the premiums or cost-sharing otherwise imposed by the amount of the subsidy.

The Act specifies that Medicare is the primary payer for covered drugs for dual eligibles. Medicaid coverage is not available for such drugs or any cost-sharing for such drugs. In 2006, states are liable for approximately 90% of the costs they would otherwise incur if drug coverage for dual eligibles continued to be offered under Medicaid; by 2015, this percentage drops to 75%.

Direct Subsidies

Federal subsidy payments will be made to qualifying entities. The stated purpose of such payments is to reduce premiums for all beneficiaries consistent with an overall subsidy level of 74% for basic coverage, reduce adverse selection among plans, and promote the participation of PDP sponsors and MA organizations. Such payments would be made as direct subsidies and through reinsurance.

The Act specifies a formula for the calculation of the direct monthly per capita subsidy amount. It is equal to the plans standardized bid amount adjusted for health status and risk and reduced by the base beneficiary premium as adjusted to reflect the difference between the bid and the national average bid. Reinsurance payments, equal to 80% of allowable costs, would also be provided for an enrollee whose costs exceeded the annual out-of-pocket threshold ($3,600 in 2006).

Risk Corridors

The Act provides for the establishment of risk corridors, which are defined as specified percentages above and below a target amount. The target amount is defined as total payments paid to the plan, taking into account the amount paid by the Secretary and enrollees, based on the standardized bid amount, risk adjusted, and reduced by total administrative expenses assumed in the bid. No payment adjustments will be made if adjusted allowable costs for the plan are at least equal to the first threshold lower limit of the first risk corridor but not greater than the first threshold upper limit of the risk corridor for the year, i.e., if the plans are within the first risk corridor. A portion of any plan spending above or below these levels is subject to risk adjustment. If adjusted allowable costs exceed the first threshold upper limit, then payments are increased. If adjusted allowable costs are below the first threshold lower limit, then payments are reduced. Adjusted allowable costs are reduced by reinsurance and subsidy payments. Payment adjustments would not affect beneficiary premiums.

During 2006 and 2007, plans will be at full risk for adjusted allowable risk corridor costs within 2.5% above or below the target. Plans with adjusted allowable costs above this level will receive increased payments. If their costs are between 2.5% of the target (first threshold upper limit) and 5% of the target (second threshold upper limit), they will be at risk for 25% of the increased amount; that is, their payments will equal 75% of adjusted allowable costs for spending in this range. If their costs are above 5% of the target they will be at risk for 25% of the costs between the first and second threshold upper limits and 20% of the costs above that amount. That is, their payments will equal 80% of the adjusted allowable costs over the second threshold upper limit. Conversely, if plans fell below the target, they will share the savings with the government. They will have to refund 75% of the savings if costs fall between 2.5% and 5% below the target level, and 80% of any amounts below 5% of the target.

A higher risk sharing percentage will apply in 2006 and 2007 if the Secretary determines that 60% of prescription drug plans and MA-PD plans, representing at least 60% of beneficiaries enrolled in such plans have adjusted allowable costs that are more than the first threshold upper limit. In this case, payment to plans would equal 90% of adjusted allowable costs between the first and second upper threshold limits.

For 2008-2011, the risk corridors will be modified. Plans will be at full risk for drug spending within 5.0% above or below the target level. Plans will be at risk for 50% of spending exceeding 5.0% and below 10.0% of the target level. Additionally, they will be at risk for 20% of any spending exceeding 10% of the target level.

Subsidies for Retiree Plans

Under certain conditions, the Secretary is required to make special subsidy payments to sponsors of qualified retiree prescription drug plans. These payments are to be made on behalf of an individual covered under the retiree plan, who is entitled to enroll under a PDP or MA-PD plan but elected not to. Subsidy payments will equal 28% of a retiree's gross covered retiree plan-related prescription drug costs over the $250 deductible but not over $5,000. (The dollar amounts would be adjusted annually by the percentage increase in Medicare per capita prescription drug costs.)

Relationship to Other Programs

The Act requires the Secretary, by July 1, 2005, to establish requirements to ensure effective coordination between a Part D plan (both a prescription drug plan and MA-PD plan) and a state pharmaceutical assistance program. The coordination requirements are to relate to payment of premiums and coverage and payment for supplemental drug benefits. Requirements must be included for enrollment file-sharing, claims processing, claims reconciliation reports, application of the catastrophic out-of-pocket protection, and other administrative procedures specified by the Secretary. Similar coordination provisions are to be applied to other prescription plans including Medicaid (including a plan operating under an 1115 waiver), group health plans, federal employees health benefits plan, military coverage (including TRICARE), and other coverage specified by the Secretary.

Medigap

The Act prohibits, effective January 1, 2006, the selling, issuance, or renewal of existing Medigap policies with prescription drug coverage for Part D enrollees. The prohibition does not apply to renewal of Medigap prescription policies for persons who are not Part D enrollees. Persons enrolling under Part D during the initial enrollment period may enroll in a Medigap plan without drug coverage, or continue their previous policy as modified to exclude drugs. Medigap issuers will be required to notify individuals of these changes 60 days prior to the initial Part D enrollment period.

Medicare Prescription Drug Discount Card

For the period prior to implementation of the new drug program, the Secretary was required to establish a temporary program to endorse prescription drug discount card programs meeting certain requirements. The purpose is to provide access to prescription drug discounts through card sponsors to persons who voluntarily enroll in the program. Each card sponsor is to provide each enrollee with access to negotiated prices. The program also provides transitional assistance for low-income persons enrolled in endorsed programs.[2]

The Act requires the Secretary to implement the program so that discount cards and transitional assistance are available no later than six months after enactment. It does not apply to covered discount card drugs dispensed after December 31, 2005. The Act specifies that persons eligible for the discount card are those entitled to or enrolled under Part A or enrolled under Part B. However, an individual enrolled in Medicaid (or under any Section 1115 Medicaid waiver) who is entitled to any medical assistance for outpatient prescribed drugs is not a discount card-eligible individual.

An individual not enrolled in a card program may enroll in any card program serving residents of the state at any time beginning on the initial enrollment date and before January 1, 2006. A discount eligible individual may only be enrolled in one endorsed card program at a time. An individual enrolled in one program in 2004 may change the election for 2005. A card sponsor may charge an annual enrollment fee, not to exceed $30.

The Act provides special provisions for low-income persons (defined as those with incomes below 135% of poverty). A transitional assistance eligible individual is entitled to have his or her discount card enrollment fee paid. Those individuals with incomes below 100% of poverty (special transitional assistance eligible individuals) are liable for coinsurance charges of 5% of incurred costs up to $600 in both 2004 and 2005. Other transitional assistance eligible individuals (those with incomes between 100% and 135% of poverty) are liable for coinsurance charges of 10 % of incurred costs up to $600 in both 2004 and 2005. Thus, the program pays 95% of a special transitional eligible individual's incurred drug costs up to $600 in 2004 and 90% of other transitional eligible individual's incurred drug costs up to $600 in 2004. Similarly, payment is made for 95% or 90%, whichever is appropriate, of the individual's incurred drug costs up to $600 in 2005. In addition, any balance left over from 2004 may be added to the amount available in 2005, except no rollover is permitted if the individual voluntarily disenrolled from an endorsed program. Certain persons are not eligible for transitional assistance. These are persons who have coverage for drugs under a group health plan, federal employees health benefits plan, or through coverage made available to members of the uniformed services.

MEDICARE ADVANTAGE

The Act establishes the Medicare Advantage (MA) program under Part C of Medicare, to replace the Medicare+Choice program. MA local plans continue to be offered as coordinated care and other plans on a county-wide basis. Beginning in 2006, in addition to the MA *local* plans, the MA program will begin to offer MA *regional* coordinated care plans that cover both in- and out-of-network required services. Beginning in 2010, the Comparative Cost Adjustment (CCA) program will be established for a six-year period, to: (1) examine a new MA payment system under which payments to MA plans would be based on a weighted average of plans bids; and (2) introduce possible adjustments (either increases or decreases) to fee-for-service Part B premiums, based on a comparison of the costs of providing required fee-for-service benefits to the costs of providing the same benefits in the MA program.

Beneficiaries in MA plans will not be required to enroll in the new prescription drug program, Part D. However, at least one plan offered by an

MA organization in an area is required to offer Part D prescription drug coverage. Therefore, if the beneficiary has only one available MA plan from which to chose, then in effect, the beneficiary must enroll in Part D in order to enroll in a plan.

Prior to the enactment of the Act, Medicare+Choice (M+C) plans were paid an administered monthly payment, called the M+C payment rate, for each enrollee. The per capita rate for a payment area was set at the highest of one of three amounts: (1) a minimum payment (or floor) rate, (2) a rate calculated as a blend of an area-specific (local) rate and a national rate, or (3) a rate reflecting a minimum increase from the previous year's rate (currently 2%).

For 2004, the Act modified payments to MA plans. First, a fourth payment mechanism was added so that plans are paid the highest of the floor, minimum percent increase, the blend, or a new amount. The new payment amount is 100% of fee-for-service (FFS) payments made for persons enrolled in traditional Medicare. The FFS payment is calculated based on the adjusted average per capita cost for the year for an MA payment area (a county), for services covered under Medicare Parts A and B for beneficiaries entitled to benefits under Part A, enrolled in Part B and not enrolled in an MA plan. Second, there was a change made to the blend payment, so that there is no adjustment for budget neutrality in 2004.[3] Third, the calculation of the minimum percentage increase was also be revised. For 2004 and beyond the minimum percentage increase is the greater of a 2% increase over the previous year's payment rate (as under current law), or the previous year's payment increased by the growth in overall Medicare for the previous year. Beginning in 2005, the statute no longer allows MA payments to be annually updated by the floor or blend. Thus only the minimum increase, and in certain years[4], 100% of per capita FFS will be used to update payment rates.

Additional changes to the MA program will be made, beginning in 2006. The Secretary will determine MA payment rates by comparing plan bids to a benchmark. Plans will submit bids for providing required Parts A and B benefits. The benchmark will be calculated by updating the previous year's capitation rate by the annual increase in the minimum percentage increase. For plans with bids below the benchmark, the payment will equal the unadjusted MA statutory non-drug monthly bid amount, as adjusted, and the rebate. The rebate will equal 75% of any average per capita savings (the amount by which the risk-adjusted benchmark exceeds the risk adjusted bid). The rebate may be used to provide additional benefits, reduce cost sharing, or may be applied towards the monthly Part B premium, prescription drug premium, or supplemental premium. The remaining 25% of the average per capita savings will be retained by the federal government. For plans with bids at or above the benchmark (for which there are no average per capita monthly savings), the payment amount will equal the FFS area-specific non-drug monthly benchmark amount, as adjusted. For the plans with bids above the benchmark, the enrollee's premium will equal the full amount by which the bid exceeds the benchmark.

Beginning in 2006, the MA program will also begin to offer MA regional coordinated care plans that cover both in- and out-of-network required services. There will be at least 10 regions established and no more than 50 regions. Each MA regional plan must offer a maximum limit on out-of-pocket expenses and a unified deductible. Each year an organization will submit a separate monthly bid amount for *each* plan it intends to offer in a region. Payments will be based on a competitive bidding system, so that the benchmark for MA regions will be calculated using a statutory formula that includes a weighted average of plan bids for the region. For plans with bids below the benchmark (for which there are average per capita monthly savings), the payment will equal the unadjusted MA regional statutory non-drug monthly bid amount, as adjusted, and the rebate. The plan will provide the enrollee a monthly rebate equal to 75% of the average per capita savings. For plans with bids at or above the benchmark (for which there are no average per capita monthly savings), the payment amount will equal the region-specific non-drug monthly benchmark amount, as adjusted. For the plans with bids above the benchmark, the enrollee's premium will be increased by the full amount by which the bid exceeds the benchmark.

The Act also establishes a stabilization fund to provide incentives for plans to enter into and to remain in the MA program. There will be $10 billion initially provided to the stabilization fund and additional amounts will be added to the fund from a portion of any average per capita monthly savings amounts.[5] The Secretary will be responsible for determining the amounts that may be given to MA plans from this fund, based on statutory requirements. For example, the national bonus payment will be available to an MA organization that offers an MA regional plan in every MA region in the year, but only if there was no national plan in the previous year.

During 2006 and 2007, Medicare will share risk with MA regional plans if plan costs fall above or below a statutorily-specified risk corridor. If the Secretary determines that a plan's allowable costs are over 103% of a specified target amount, the plan will receive an additional payment. Conversely, if a regional plan's allowable costs are under 97% of the specified target amount, the plan will receive a decrease in its payment.

The Act requires the Secretary to establish a program for the application of comparative cost adjustment (CCA) in CCA areas. The six-year CCA program begins January 1, 2010 and ends December 31, 2015. The CCA program is designed to examine the efficiency of private plans in the Medicare program verses traditional Medicare. For that purpose: (1) payments to local MA plans would be based on competitive bids (similar to payments for the regional MA plans), and (2) premiums for individuals enrolled in traditional Medicare could be adjusted, either up of down. Upon completion of the CCA program, the Secretary will submit a report to Congress that evaluates the cost of the program, provider access, beneficiary satisfaction and recommendations for any extension or expansions.

The Secretary will select CCA areas from among those Metropolitan Statistical Areas (MSA), or such similar area as the Secretary recognizes, that meet certain requirements. The requirements for an MSA to qualify as a CCA include: (1) for the reference month in 2010 (defined as the most recent month during the previous year for which the Secretary determines that data are available to compute the relevant calculation) at least 25% of MA eligible individuals who reside in the MSA are enrolled in an MA local plan; and (2) before the beginning of 2010, at least two MA local plans will be offered by different organizations in the MSA during the annual coordinated election period, each meeting the current law minimum enrollment requirements for a plan, as of the reference month. The number of MSAs selected may not exceed the lesser of six sites or 25% of the number of MSAs meeting the requirements. Additionally, an MA local area (a county) in an MSA will be excluded from the CCA area, if, in 2010, it does not offer at least two MA local plans, each offered by a different MA organization.

Payments will be based on a competitive bidding system, so that the benchmark for CCA areas will be calculated using a statutory formula that includes a weighted average of plan bids for the area. Similar to the rebates under the MA program, beneficiaries in CCA areas will receive a rebate, equal to 75% of the average per capita monthly savings, for plans with bids below the CCA benchmark. For plans with bids above the benchmark, the enrollee's premium will be equal to the full amount by which the bid exceeds the benchmark. The CCA program is phased in through 2013. During the first year of the phase-in, 2010, the benchmark is one-fourth CCA benchmark and three-fourths non-CCA benchmark, increasing the CCA share by another one-fourth each year until the benchmark is 100% CCA.

The CCA program will introduce competition between traditional FFS Medicare and local private plans. As a result, an individual residing in a CCA area who is enrolled in Part B of Medicare, but not enrolled in an MA plan, can have an adjustment to his or her Part B premium, either as an increase or a decrease. No premium adjustment will be made for individuals, for a month that they are a subsidy eligible individual (those individuals qualifying for a subsidy under the Part D prescription drug program). The Part B premium adjustment for FFS beneficiaries in CCA areas will be made as follows: (1) if the FFS area-specific non-drug amount for the month *does not exceed* the CCA non-drug benchmark, the Part B premium is reduced by 75% of the difference; and (2) if the FFS area-specific non-drug amount for the month *exceeds* the CCA non-drug benchmark, the Part B premium is increased by the full amount of the difference. This adjustment will be phased-in over four years. There is also a 5% annual limit on the adjustment, so that the amount of the adjustment for a year, can not exceed 5% of the amount of the monthly Part B premium, as otherwise determined.

CBO estimates that over the 10-year period FY2004-FY2013, direct spending will be increased by $14.2 billion for the provisions of Title II. Of that total, $14.1 billion will be for payments to MA plans and $0.4 for other provisions. Offsetting those costs, CBO estimates savings from the CCA program's payments to plans of $0.3 billion.

COST CONTAINMENT

The Act requires the President to propose and Congress to consider legislation to address Medicare spending any time general revenue funding[6] of Medicare is projected to exceed 45% in two consecutive years. Specifically, the Medicare Board of Trustees of the Hospital Insurance Trust Fund (Part A) and the Supplementary Medical Insurance Trust Fund (Part B) are required to include the their annual reports a determination as to whether "excess general revenue medicare funding" exceeds 45%. Excess general revenue Medicare funding is general revenue Medicare funding (defined as total Medicare outlays minus dedicated Medicare financing) expressed as a percentage of total Medicare outlays. For the purposes of this provision, total Medicare outlays are defined as total outlays from the Medicare trust funds and includes Medicare administrative expenditures. Dedicated Medicare financing includes Medicare payroll taxes, premiums for Part A[7], Part B, and Part D, transfers from the Railroad Retirement accounts, taxation of certain OASDI benefits, state transfers for Medicare coverage of beneficiaries who receive public assistance, and gifts[8].

Beginning with their report in 2005, the Trustees' annual report is required to include information on: (1) projections of growth of general revenue Medicare spending as a percentage of the total Medicare outlays for each year within a seven-fiscal-year timeframe, and 10, 50, and 75 years after the fiscal; (2) comparisons with the growth trends for the gross domestic product, private health costs, national health expenditures, and other appropriate measures; (3) expenditures and trends in expenditures under Part D; and (4) a financial analysis of the combined Medicare Part A and Part B trust funds if general revenue funding for Medicare were limited to 45% of total Medicare outlays. The Trustees reports are also required to include a determination as to whether there is projected to be "excess general revenue Medicare funding" for any of the succeeding six fiscal years in their annual reports of Medicare's trust funds.

An affirmative determination of excess general revenue funding of Medicare for two consecutive annual reports will be treated as funding warning for Medicare in the second year for the purposes of the President's budget content and submission to Congress. Whenever any Trustees report includes a determination that within the seven-fiscal-year timeframe that there is excess general revenue Medicare funding, the President is required to submit to Congress proposed legislation to respond to the warning. Procedures and timeframes for House and Senate consideration of the legislation are prescribed.

ADMINISTRATION OF MEDICARE PART C AND PART D

The Medicare program is administered by the Centers for Medicare & Medicaid Services (CMS) within the Department of Health and Human Services (HHS). Both the House and Senate bills would have established a new agency to administer Medicare Advantage, and Part D, prescription drugs within HHS but separate from CMS. In the Act, a new Center for Beneficiary Services within CMS is established to administer Medicare Advantage, the prescription drug benefit, and beneficiary information activities.

APPEALS, REGULATORY, AND CONTRACTING PROVISIONS

The Act contains numerous provisions addressing Medicare appeals, regulatory relief, and contracting reform. Specifically, the Act modifies the way Medicare regulations and guidance are communicated; modifies the procedures used to resolve payment disputes; and establishes various provider appeal processes, particularly for those who face termination of Medicare participation or denial of their application to participate in the program. The Act refines the information required to be provided in the appeals process and makes other modifications. The administrative law judge (ALJ) function for Medicare hearings is required to be transferred from the Social Security Administration (SSA) to HHS, no later than October 1, 2005. The Act gives the Secretary the authority to competitively contract for claims processing services with any qualified entities; requires these contracts to be competitively bid at least every five years; and places new requirements on the Medicare claims processing contractors, including an increased emphasis on provider education. Other program changes, demonstration projects, and mandated studies are also included in the Act. The Act authorizes increased funding but action by the appropriations committees is required for CMS to receive additional money.

PROVISIONS AFFECTING MEDICARE'S FEE-FOR-SERVICE PROGRAM PAYMENTS, DEMONSTRATION PROJECTS, EXPANSION OF COVERED BENEFITS AND BENEFICIARY COST SHARING

Changes to Medicare's Fee-for-Service Program [9]

The Act contains extensive changes to Medicare's fee-for-service (FFS) program, including payment increases and, in certain instances, decreases; development of competitive acquisition programs; implementation or refinement of other prospective payment systems (notably, the development of an end-stage renal disease (ESRD) basic payment system); expansion of covered preventive benefits; establishment of demonstration programs; and required studies. The anticipated financial impact of these changes on any individual provider, physician, or supplier will vary depending on many factors, such as the unique characteristics of the individual or entity participating in Medicare as well as the number and type of services provided to the Medicare beneficiaries they serve. Selected highlights of the FFS payment provisions and those establishing preventive care benefits and demonstration programs will be briefly described.

Selected Rural Provider Provisions

Generally, Medicare payments to certain rural providers increase; many of the rural provisions benefit urban providers as well. CBO estimated that the rural provisions in Title IV of the Act increase Medicare's direct spending by $9.3 billion from 2004 through 2008 and by $19.9 billion from 2004 though 2013. It should be noted that other provider payment provisions in the law can impact rural providers, but their cost implications for rural providers is unclear.

Rural Hospitals. Rural hospitals (and hospitals in small urban areas) receive an permanent 1.6% increase to Medicare's base rate or per discharge payment; the limit on rural and small urban hospitals that qualify for disproportionate share hospital (DSH) payments increases from 5.25% to 12%; hospitals in low wage areas (those with wage index values below 1) receive additional payments through a decrease from 71% to 62% in the labor-related portion of the base payment rate; certain small rural hospitals with less than 50 beds (those in newly established scarcity areas) receive cost reimbursement for outpatient clinical laboratory tests; rural hospitals with less than 100 beds are protected from payment declines associated with the hospital outpatient prospective payment system (OPPS) for an additional two years; these OPPS hold harmless provisions are extended to sole community hospitals for services from 2004 through 2006. CBO estimated that these provisions increase direct Medicare spending by $15.6 billion over the 10-year period.

Critical Access Hospitals. Critical access hospitals (CAHs) have their bed limit increased from 15 to 25; there is no restriction on the number of these beds that can be used for acute care services at any one time; CAHs are able to establish distinct part rehabilitation and psychiatric units of up to 10 beds that will not be included in the CAH bed count; cost reimbursement of CAH services increased to 101% of reasonable costs, starting January 1, 2004; periodic interim payments for CAHs are authorized; state authority to waive the 35-mile requirement for new entities to qualify as a CAH will be eliminated as of January 1, 2006. CBO estimated that these provisions increase direct Medicare spending by $900 million over the 10-year period.

Rural Physicians. Rural physicians in newly established scarcity areas receive a 5% increase in Medicare payments in 2005, 2006, and 2007; physicians in certain low-cost areas with geographic adjustment factors below 1 receive payment increases so as to increase this factor to 1, starting in 2004 through 2006. CBO estimated that these provisions will increase direct Medicare spending by $1.7 billion over the 10-year period.

Rural Practitioners. Rural practitioners in rural health clinics and federally qualified health centers can bill separately for services provided to beneficiaries in skilled nursing facilities. CBO estimated that these provisions increase direct Medicare spending by $100 million over the 10-year period.

Rural Home Health Providers. Rural home health providers received a 5% increase in Medicare payments for one year beginning April 1, 2004. CBO estimated that this one-year increase will increase direct Medicare spending by $100 million over the 10-year period.

Selected Acute Hospital Provisions

Generally, Medicare payments to hospitals increase under the law. Acute hospitals paid under the inpatient prospective payment system (IPPS) that submit data on specified quality indicators will receive a full update from 2005 through 2007; those hospitals that do not submit such data will receive an update minus 0.4 percentage points for the year in question. CBO expected that this latter provision will reduce direct spending 0.2 billion from 2004 through 2008. Teaching hospitals will receive an increase of an expected $400 million in their indirect medical education payments from 2004 through 2006. A one-time, geographic reclassification process to increase hospitals' wage index values for three years that was expected to increase payments by $900 million from 2004 through 2008 was established. Low volume hospitals with fewer than 800 discharges that are 25 road miles away from a similar hospital may qualify for up to a 25% increase in its Medicare payments. Changes to outpatient hospital payments for covered drugs were expected to increase payments by $700 million from FY2004 through FY2008. A redistribution of unused resident positions increase both direct and indirect graduate medical education spending by an anticipated $200 million from FY2004 thought FY2008 and by $600 million from FY2004 through FY2013. Certain teaching hospitals with high per resident payments will not receive a payment increase from FY2004 through FY2013; this provision was scored by CBO as a reduction in Medicare spending of $500 million from FY2004 through FY2008 and $1.3 billion from FY2004 through FY2013. For 18 months from the date of enactment, physicians can not to refer Medicare patients to specialty hospitals in which they have an investment interest. This provision does not apply to hospitals that are in operation or under development before November 18, 2003. Both MedPAC and HHS are to complete required studies on specialty hospitals within 15 months of enactment.

Selected Physician Provisions

The impact of the Act on Medicare's spending for physician spending is difficult to determine. Although physicians receive a 1.5% update in 2004 and 2005 which is expected to increase spending by $2.8 billion from FY2004 through FY2007; subsequently, from FY2008 through FY2012, the provision is expected to result in a decline of $2.8 billion in Medicare spending. Medicare's payments for practice expenses, particularly the administration of covered drugs, increased starting in 2004. A transitional adjustment to the drug administration payments of 32% in 2004 and 3% in 2005 was also established. These payment increases were expected to be counterbalanced by a decrease in Medicare's payments for covered outpatient drugs provided in a doctor's office. Many covered outpatient drugs furnished in 2004 are reimbursed at 85% of the average wholesale price (AWP), with certain of these drugs paid as low as 80% of the AWP (as of April 1, 2003). Blood clotting factors and other blood products, drugs or biologicals (drug products) that were not available for payment by April 1, 2003, covered vaccinations, drug products furnished in during 2004 in connection with renal dialysis services, drugs provided through covered durable medical equipment are paid at a higher rate during 2004. The decline in payments for covered outpatient drugs in 2004 could only be implemented concurrently with the increased payments for the administration of the drugs. Starting in 2005, Medicare's payment for many covered outpatient drugs is based on average sales price methodology, that uses different pricing and cost data, depending on the prescription drug. Generally, multiple source drugs are paid 106% of the average sales price; single source drugs are paid 106% of the lower of the average sales price or the wholesale acquisition costs, unless the widely available market price or the average manufacturer price for those drugs exceeds a certain threshold. Starting in 2006, physicians will have the option of obtaining covered Part B drugs from selected entities awarded contracts for competitively biddable drug products under the newly established competitive acquisition program.

Selected Provisions Affecting Other Providers and Practitioners

The follow provisions affecting other providers and practitioners are included in the legislation:

Ambulatory Surgical Centers. Payments to ambulatory surgical centers (ASCs) are expected to be lower by $800 million from FY2004 through FY2008 and by $3.1 billion from FY2004 through FY2013 as a result of the legislation. ASCs received an update of the consumer price index for all urban consumers (CPI-U) minus 3.0 percentage points starting April 1, 2004 and receive a 0% update for services provided starting October 1, 2004 through December 31, 2009.

Therapy Caps. Application of the caps on outpatient therapy services provided by non-hospital providers was suspended for the remainder of 2003, in 2004 and 2005. CBO estimated that the therapy cap moratorium will increase direct Medicare spending by $700 million over the 10-year period.

Durable Medical Equipment (DME). Competitive bidding for DME will be phased in beginning in 2007 with 10 of the largest metropolitan statistical areas and may be phased in first among the highest cost and highest volume items and services. The update for most DME items and services and for prosthetics and orthotics is 0 in 2004, 2005, 2006, 2007, and 2008. For 2005, payment for certain items, oxygen and oxygen equipment, standard wheelchairs, nebulizers, diabetic lancets and testing strips, hospital beds and air mattresses are reduced by an amount calculated using 2002 payment amounts and specified payment amounts by FEHP. Beginning January 1, 2009, items and services included in the competitive acquisition program will be paid as determined under that program and the Secretary can use this information to adjust the payment amounts for DME, off-the-shelf orthotics, and other items and services that are supplied in an area that is not a competitive acquisition area. Class III items (devices that sustain or support life, are implanted, or present potential unreasonable risk, e.g., implantable infusion pumps and heart valve replacements, and are subject to premarket approval, the most stringent regulatory control) receive the full increase in the consumer price index for all urban consumers (CPI-U) in 2004, 2005, 2006 , 2008 and subsequent year. The Secretary will determine the update in 2007. CBO scored the DME provisions of the bill as reducing spending by $6.8 billion over the 10-year period.

Home Health. Home health agency payments were increased by the full market basket percentage for the last quarter of 2003 (October, November, and December) and for the first quarter of 2004 (January, February, and March). The update for the remainder of 2004 and for 2005 and 2006 is the home health market basket percentage increase minus 0.8 percentage points. CBO estimated that this provision will reduce direct Medicare spending by $6.5 billion over the 10-year period. The Act suspended the requirement that home health agencies must collect OASIS data on private pay (non-Medicare, non-Medicaid) until the Secretary reports to Congress and publishes final regulations regarding the collection and use of OASIS.

Selected Fee-for Service Demonstration Projects

The Act establishes numerous demonstration projects for the Medicare program. Several demonstrations address aspects of disease management for beneficiaries with chronic conditions.

Chronic Care Improvement under Fee-for-Service. The Act requires the Secretary to establish and implement chronic care improvement programs under fee-for-service Medicare to improve clinical quality and beneficiary satisfaction and achieve spending targets for Medicare for beneficiaries with certain chronic health conditions. Participation by beneficiaries is voluntary. The contractors are required to assume financial risk for performance under the contract. CBO estimated that this demonstration will increase direct Medicare spending by $500 million over the 10-year period.

Chronically Ill Beneficiary Research, Demonstration. The Act requires the Secretary to develop a plan to improve quality of care and to reduce the cost of care for chronically ill Medicare beneficiaries within six months after enactment. The plan is required to use existing data and identify data gaps, develop research initiatives, and propose intervention demonstration programs to provide better health care for chronically ill Medicare beneficiaries. The Secretary is required to implement the plan no later than two years after enactment.

Coverage of Certain Drugs and Biologicals Demonstration. The Secretary is required by the Act to conduct a two-year demonstration where payment is made for certain drugs and biologicals that are currently provided as "incident to" a physician's services under Part B. The demonstration is required to provide for cost-sharing in the same manner as applies under Part D of Medicare. The demonstration is required to begin within 90 days of enactment and is limited to 50,000 Medicare beneficiaries in sites selected by the Secretary.

Homebound Demonstration. The Secretary is required to conduct a two-year demonstration project where beneficiaries with chronic conditions would be deemed to be homebound in order to receive home health services under Medicare.

Adult Day Care. The Secretary is required to establish a demonstration where beneficiaries could receive adult day care services as a substitute for a portion of home health services otherwise provided in a beneficiary's home.

Expansion of Covered Benefits

The Act contains a number of provisions that expand coverage beginning January 1, 2005, including the following:

Initial Physical Examination. Medicare coverage of an initial preventive physical examination is authorized for those individuals whose Medicare coverage begins on or after January 1, 2005. CBO estimated that this provision will increase direct Medicare spending by $1.7 billion over the 10-year period.

Cardiovascular Screening Blood Tests. Medicare coverage of cardiovascular screening blood tests is authorized. CBO estimated that this provision will increase direct Medicare spending by $300 million over the 10-year period.

Diabetes Screening Tests. Diabetes screening tests furnished to an individual at risk for diabetes for the purpose of early detection of diabetes are included as a covered medical service. In this instance, diabetes screening tests include fasting plasma glucose tests as well as other tests and modifications to those tests deemed appropriate by the Secretary. CBO estimated that this provision will increase direct Medicare spending less than $50 million over the 10-year period.

Screening and Diagnostic Mammography. Screening mammography and diagnostic mammography are excluded from OPPS and paid separately. CBO estimated that this provision will increase direct Medicare spending by $200 million over the 10-year period.

Intravenous Immune Globulin. The Act includes intravenous immune globulin for the treatment in the home of primary immune deficiency diseases as a covered medical service under Medicare. CBO estimated that this provision will increase direct Medicare spending by $100 million over the 10-year period.

BENEFICIARY COST SHARING IN FEE-FOR-SERVICE

The Act contains two provisions changing beneficiary cost sharing responsibilities under fee-for-service Medicare.

Income Relating to the Part B Premium

The Act increases the monthly Part B premiums for higher-income enrollees beginning in 2007. Beneficiaries whose modified adjusted gross income exceed $80,000 and couples filing joint returns whose modified adjusted gross income exceeds $160,000 will be subject to higher premium amounts. The increase will be calculated on a sliding scale basis and will be phased-in over a five-year period. The highest category on the sliding scale is for beneficiaries whose modified adjusted gross income is more than $200,000 ($400,000 for a couple filing jointly). CBO estimated that direct Medicare spending will be reduced by $13.3 billion over the 10-year period 2004 through 2013.

Indexing the Part B Deductible

The Medicare Part B deductible remained $100 through 2004, increases to $110 for 2005, and in subsequent years the deductible will be increased by the same percentage as the Part B premium increase. Specifically, the annual percentage increase in the monthly actuarial value of benefits payable from the Federal Supplementary Medical Insurance Trust Fund will be used as the index.

MEDICAID AND MISCELLANEOUS PROVISIONS

Title X of the Act makes some changes to Medicaid and other programs. Omitted from the Act were two provisions contained in S. 1, including a provision to amend the Age Discrimination in Employment Act of 1967 to allow an employee benefit plan to offer different benefits to their Medicare eligible employees than to their non-Medicare eligible employees, and a provision to allow states to cover certain lawfully residing aliens under the Medicaid program.

CBO estimated the Medicaid and other provisions included in the law will increase direct spending by $5.7 billion between FY2004 and FY2013. The following general points can be made about the Medicaid and Miscellaneous provisions included in Title X of the Act:

- The Act temporarily increases states' disproportionate share hospital (DSH) allotments to erase the decline in these Medicaid amounts that occurred after a special rule for their calculation expired.
- The Act includes several other Medicaid provisions, including raising the floor on DSH allotments for "extremely low DSH states," providing DSH allotment adjustments impacting Hawaii and/or Tennessee, increasing reporting requirements for

DSH hospitals, and exempting prices of drugs provided to certain safety net hospitals from Medicaid's best price drug program.
- Miscellaneous provisions in Title X of the Act include funding federal reimbursement of emergency health services furnished to ndocumented aliens, and funding administrative start-up costs for

Medicare reform, various research projects, work groups and infrastructure improvement programs for the health care system.

TAX INCENTIVES FOR HEALTH AND RETIREMENT SECURITY

Title XII of the Act authorizes new tax-advantaged accounts for medical expenses called health savings accounts (HSAs). These accounts are similar to the medical savings accounts (MSAs) that were authorized by the Health Insurance Portability and Accountability Act of 1996 (P.L. 104-191), but they will be more widely available and have more generous contribution limits. As is the case with MSAs, unused balances can be carried over from year to year. Contributions to HSAs may be made when individuals have qualifying high deductible medical insurance and no other health insurance, with some exceptions; in 2004, the insurance deductible for self-only coverage must be at least $1,000 (rather than $1,700 for MSAs) while for family coverage it must be at least $2,000 (rather than $3,450 for MSAs). In 2004, contributions are limited to the lesser of the insurance deductible or $2,600 for self-only coverage and $5,150 for family coverage; individuals who are at least 55 years of age but not yet 65 can contribute more. Unlike MSAs, HSAs may be offered through an employer's cafeteria plan. The Joint Committee on Taxation estimates that the revenue loss attributable to HSAs for FY2004 through FY2013 will be $6.4 billion.

Title XII of the Act also includes a provision allowing employers to exclude from gross income the Medicare subsidy payments they receive to maintain prescription drug coverage for their retirees. The Joint Committee on Taxation estimates that the revenue loss attributable to this exclusion for FY2004 through FY2013 will be $17.8 billion.

The Act does not include two tax provisions that had been in the House bill, one authorizing health savings security accounts (HSSAs) and another allowing up to $500 in unused benefits in health care flexible spending arrangements to be rolled over to the following year or to an HSA, HSSA, or certain qualified retirement plans.

REFERENCES

[1] See [ftp://ftp.cbo.gov/48xx/doc4808/11-20-MedicareLetter.pdf] for cost estimate.

[2] For a discussion of the card program, see CRS Report RL32283, *Medicare Endorsed Prescription Drug Discount Card Program,* by Jennifer O'Sullivan.

[3] Under current law, a budget neutrality adjustment is made so that estimated total M+C payments in a given year will be equal to the total payments that would be made if payments were based solely on area-specific rates. The budget neutrality adjustment may only be applied to the blended rates, because rates cannot be reduced below the floor or minimum increase amounts.

[4] [The Secretary must rebase, or update, 100% of FFS at least once every three years, but could also choose to update more often. In years in which the Secretary does not rebase FFS payments, MA payments would be based on the minimum update only.

[5] Beneficiaries receive 75% of average per capita savings in the form of a rebate. The federal government retains the remaining 25% of the average per capita savings and one-half of the amount retained by the federal government is available to the stabilization fund.

[6] Currently, 75% of the Part B trust fund financing comes from general revenues; the remaining 25% comes from beneficiary premiums that beneficiaries voluntarily pay to enroll in Medicare Part B. The 2003 monthly premium is $58.70. The Part A trust fund revenues come primarily from payroll taxes. Employers and employees each pay 1.45% of the employees earnings, while self-employed workers pay 2.9% of their net income. Other HI revenue sources include interest on the investments of the trust fund, federal income taxes on Social Security benefits, premiums from voluntary enrollees into Part A, railroad retirement account transfers and reimbursement for certain uninsured persons.

[7] A small number of Medicare beneficiaries are not entitled to Part A but are eligible to purchase the Part A benefit by paying monthly premiums, currently $316 per month.

[8] Excluded from the list is interest on the Part A trust fund. According to the Medicare Trustees 2002 report, this amounted to approximately 7.7% of the revenue to the trust fund in 2002.

[9] For a detailed discussion of these provisions, see CRS Report RL32005, *Medicare Fee-for-Service Modifications and Medicaid Provisions of H.R. 1 as Enacted*, by Sibyl Tilson et al.

In: Health Care Crisis in America
Editor: Janet B. Prince, pp. 45-75

ISBN: 1-59454-689-4
© 2006 Nova Science Publishers, Inc.

Chapter 3

PRESCRIPTION DRUG IMPORTATION AND INTERNET SALES: A LEGAL OVERVIEW[*]

Jody Feder

SUMMARY

As prescription drug prices have escalated in recent years, so too has consumer interest in purchasing less costly medications abroad. Meanwhile, in July, 2003, the House of Representatives passed H.R. 2427, a bill that would allow wholesalers, pharmacists, and consumers to import certain prescription drugs from 25 different countries, including Canada, where drug prices are often lower than in the United States. Although H.R. 2427 passed the House, the provisions allowing drug importation faced opposition in the Senate and were not included in the conference agreement on Medicare prescription drug benefits. Instead, the final Medicare bill, H.R. 1, modified a provision of existing law that authorizes the Food and Drug Administration (FDA) to allow the importation of prescription drugs if the Secretary of Health and Human Services certifies that implementing such a program is safe and reduces costs, a determination that no Secretary has made in the years since a similar certification requirement was established in 2000.

Despite the compromise reached in the final Medicare bill, the debate about drug importation continues. On the one hand, the FDA and some lawmakers remain opposed to allowing prescription drugs to be imported

---

[*] Excerpted from CRS Report for Congress RL32191, January 8, 2004.

from foreign countries, arguing that the FDA cannot guarantee the safety of such drugs. On the other hand, importation proponents, who claim that importation would result in significantly lower prices for U.S. consumers, say that safety concerns are overblown and would recede if additional precautions were implemented.

Just as the FDA has expressed concerns about the safety of imported drugs, federal regulators have become increasingly worried about the risks posed by some online pharmacies and Internet drug sales. Indeed, the regulation of prescription drug importation and the oversight of online pharmacies often overlap because many consumers use online pharmacies to purchase imported drugs. Regardless of whether or not drugs purchased online are imported, the FDA is worried about the safety of such medications because of its concern that a small number of online doctors and pharmacies are exploiting regulatory gaps to prescribe and dispense illegal, addictive, or unsafe drugs.

In response to concerns about prescription drug imports and Internet sales, several congressional lawmakers have introduced the following bills: H.R. 616, H.R. 780, H.R. 847, H.R. 2497, H.R. 2652, H.R. 2717, H.R. 2769, S. 1781, S. 1974, and S. 1992. Currently, the following federal and state agencies are involved in regulating aspects of prescription drug importation and Internet sales: the Food and Drug Administration, the U.S. Customs and Border Protection (CBP), the Drug Enforcement Agency (DEA), state boards of pharmacy, and state medical boards. Although this article is intended to focus on legal aspects of prescription drug importation and Internet sales, both legal and policy issues are addressed because they are closely linked.

PRESCRIPTION DRUG IMPORTATION AND INTERNET SALES: A LEGAL OVERVIEW

This article explores the legal issues raised by prescription drug importation and Internet sales. Although this article is intended to focus on legal analysis, both legal and policy issues are addressed because they are closely linked.

I. INTRODUCTION

As prescription drug prices have escalated in recent years, so too has consumer interest in purchasing less costly medications abroad. Meanwhile, congressional legislators have been exploring a variety of legislative solutions to the problems posed by rising drug costs. In July, 2003, the House of Representatives passed H.R. 2427, a bill that would allow wholesalers, pharmacists, and consumers to import prescription drugs that are approved by the Food and Drug Administration (FDA) and that are manufactured in FDA-approved plants. Under the bill, drugs could be imported from 25 different countries, including Canada, where drug prices are often lower than in the United States. Despite opposition from the leadership, H.R. 2427 easily passed the House, but the provisions allowing drug importation faced opposition in the Senate and were not included in the conference agreement on Medicare prescription drug benefits. Instead, the final Medicare bill, H.R. 1, modified a provision of existing law that authorizes the FDA to allow the importation of prescription drugs if the Secretary of Health and Human Services (HHS) certifies that implementing such a program is safe and reduces costs, a determination that no Secretary has made in the years since a similar certification requirement was established in 2000.[1]

Despite the fact that the final Medicare bill did not make it easier to import prescription drugs from Canada and other foreign countries, the debate about drug importation continues. On the one hand, the FDA and some lawmakers remain opposed to allowing prescription drugs to be imported from foreign countries. Worried about the risk to consumers, these critics argue that the FDA cannot guarantee the safety of such drugs,[2] which they contend are more susceptible to being mishandled, mislabeled, unapproved, or counterfeited than drugs sold domestically.

In addition, drug manufacturers and other opponents argue that allowing the importation or reimportation of prescription drugs would stifle investment in the research and development of new drugs.[3] On the other hand, importation proponents, who claim that importation would result in significantly lower prices for U.S. consumers, say that safety concerns are overblown and would recede if additional precautions were implemented. Arguing that drug manufacturers are actually concerned about their profits and not about consumer safety, proponents of importation contend that U.S. consumers should not subsidize the cost of research and development and that consumers in other countries should share the burden.[4]

Linked to the issue of prescription drug importation is a debate about drug costs. While some comparisons of U.S. and Canadian drug prices conclude that U.S. prices are up to 70 percent higher than their Canadian counterparts,[5] other studies conclude that Canadian prices are actually slightly higher than U.S. prices when adjusted for per capita income.[6] In addition, there is an unresolved debate about whether allowing drug imports would affect drug prices, with supporters arguing that drug prices would drop due to competition if imports were allowed and opponents arguing that increased demand for imported drugs and moves by manufacturers to limit supplies of cheaper drugs would cause prices to rise both in the U.S. and abroad.[7]

Just as the FDA has expressed concerns about the safety of imported drugs, federal regulators have become increasingly worried about the risks posed by some online pharmacies and prescription drug sales over the Internet. Indeed, the regulation of prescription drug importation and the oversight of online pharmacies often overlap because many consumers use online pharmacies to purchase imported drugs. Regardless of whether or not drugs purchased online are imported, the FDA is worried about the safety of such medications because of its concern about the lack of adequate physician supervision, the prospects for tampering with or counterfeiting such drugs, and the possibility that such drugs may be handled, dispensed, packaged, or shipped incorrectly.[8]

In response to concerns about prescription drug imports and Internet sales, a number of congressional legislators have introduced bills that would make changes to existing law in these areas. In addition to H.R. 2427, several other bills – including H.R. 616, H.R. 780, H.R. 847, H.R. 2497, H.R. 2717, H.R. 2769, S. 1781, S. 1974, and S. 1992 – would amend current importation policy, and at least three bills – H.R. 616, H.R. 2652, and H.R. 2717 – would make changes to the law governing how drugs are sold online.

Current regulation of prescription drug importation and Internet sales consists of a patchwork of federal and state laws in an array of areas.[9] At the federal level, the Food and Drug Agency (FDA) regulates prescription drugs under the Federal Food, Drug, and Cosmetic Act (FFDCA), which governs, among other things, the safety and efficacy of prescription medications, including the approval, manufacturing, and distribution of such drugs.[10] It is the FFDCA that prohibits the importation or reimportation of certain prescription drugs by anyone other than the manufacturer and that requires that prescription drugs may be dispensed only with a valid prescription.[11] Meanwhile, U.S. Customs and Border Protection (CBP) has the initial responsibility for examining imported goods at the nation's borders and for detaining any FDA-regulated products that appear to pose a health risk. In addition, the Drug Enforcement Agency (DEA) administers the Controlled Substances Act, which is a federal statute that establishes criminal and civil sanctions for the unlawful possession, manufacturing, or distribution of certain addictive or dangerous substances, including certain prescription drugs that share these properties, such as narcotics and opiates.[12] At the state level, state boards of pharmacy regulate pharmacy practice, and state medical boards oversee the practice of medicine. Thus, some of the laws that govern online pharmacies and doctors vary from state to state.

II. PRESCRIPTION DRUG IMPORTATION: LEGAL REGULATION

At the federal level, the FDA regulates prescription drugs under the Federal Food, Drug, and Cosmetic Act (FFDCA), which governs, among other things, the safety and efficacy of prescription medications, including the approval, manufacturing, and distribution of such drugs.[13] Although many states also have their own laws that regulate drug safety, the FDA maintains primary responsibility for overseeing prescription drugs in the United States, while the DEA and CBP have somewhat more limited regulatory authority over prescription drugs.

The FFDCA contains several provisions that apply to prescription drug imports. First, the statute contains an outright prohibition that forbids anyone other than the U.S. manufacturer from reimporting prescription drugs. This prohibition therefore affects drugs that originally are made in the U.S. Second, the FFDCA contains a number of other provisions relating to drug approvals and labeling that make it nearly impossible for prescription drugs made for foreign markets to comply with the extensive statutory requirements. These provisions generally affect foreign versions of drugs that are approved for domestic sale.

Both reimportation of U.S.-manufactured prescription drugs and importation of unapproved foreign versions of U.S.-approved prescription drugs are discussed in this section, as are the penalties under the FFDCA, the FDA's Personal Importation policy, state plans to import prescription drugs, and businesses that facilitate the importation of prescription drugs.

Reimportation

Currently, the FFDCA prohibits anyone other than the U.S. manufacturer of a prescription drug from reimporting that drug into the United States.[14] Thus, it is technically a violation of the statute for individual consumers or online pharmacies to reimport a prescription drug back into the country, even though the drug was, prior to export, originally manufactured in the U.S. and even if the drug otherwise complies with the FFDCA.[15] Although critics of this law argue that there is no rational justification for forbidding the reimportation of a drug that is theoretically identical to its counterpart sold in the U.S., the FDA contends that the agency can no longer guarantee the safety of a prescription drug once it has left the country and the agency's regulatory control. According to the agency, the FDA "cannot provide adequate assurance to the American public that the drug products delivered to consumers in the United States from foreign countries are the same products approved by the FDA."[16]

In response to concerns about the rising costs of prescription drugs, however, Congress adopted importation amendments to the FFDCA in 2000. Under the Medicine Equity and Drug Safety (MEDS) Act,[17] the FDA was authorized to allow pharmacists and wholesalers to import prescription drugs from foreign countries if certain safety precautions were followed.[18] The Act, however, stipulated that the importation provision would not become effective until and unless the Secretary of HHS determined that the implementation of the provision would "pose no additional risk to the public's health and safety; and [would] result in a significant reduction in the cost of covered products to the American consumer."[19] Citing safety concerns, both the current and the former Secretaries declined to implement this provision.

In the recently enacted Medicare Prescription Drug, Improvement, and Modernization Act of 2003 (hereinafter referred to as the Medicare Act),[20] Congress once again revisited the issue of prescription drug importation. Like the MEDS Act it superseded, the Medicare legislation directs the FDA to allow pharmacists and wholesalers to import prescription drugs if certain safety precautions are followed. Unlike the MEDS Act, which covered prescription drugs from a specified group of foreign countries, the Medicare Act allows imports from Canada only.[21] In addition, the Medicare Act, unlike the MEDS Act, also authorizes the FDA to allow, by regulatory waiver, individuals to import prescription drugs for personal use under certain circumstances.[22] Despite these new importation provisions, the Medicare Act, like the MEDS Act, stipulates that the importation provisions will not become effective until and unless the Secretary certifies that the implementation of the provision would "pose no additional risk to the public's health and safety; and [would] result in a significant reduction in the cost of covered products to the American consumer."[23] As noted above, the Secretary of HHS has thus far declined to provide such certification. Absent such certification, the ban on the importation and reimportation of prescription drugs remains in effect.

Importation of Foreign Versions of Prescription Drugs

Even if the FFDCA did not contain an explicit prohibition against drug reimportation, the FDA maintains that consumer imports of prescription drugs from foreign countries would almost certainly violate other provisions of the Act.[24] For example, such drugs are likely to be unapproved,[25] mislabeled,[26] or improperly dispensed.[27] According to the FDA:

The reason that Canadian or other foreign versions of U.S.-approved drugs are generally considered unapproved in the U.S. is that FDA approvals are manufacturer-specific, product-specific, and include many requirements relating to the product, such as manufacturing location, formulation, source and specifications of active ingredients, processing methods, manufacturing controls, container/closure system, and appearance. . . . Moreover, even if the manufacturer has FDA approval for a drug, the version produced for foreign markets usually does not meet all of the requirements of the U.S. approval, and thus it is considered to be unapproved. Virtually all shipments of prescription drugs imported from a Canadian pharmacy will run afoul of the Act, although it is a theoretical possibility that an occasional shipment will not do so. Put differently, in order to ensure compliance with the Act when they are involved in shipping prescription drugs to consumers in the U.S., businesses and individuals must ensure, among other things, that they only sell FDA-approved drugs that are made outside of the U.S. and that comply with the FDA approval in all respects.[28]

In addition to complying with the requirements regarding FDA approvals, imported drugs must also meet FDA requirements regarding labeling and dispensing. For example, mislabeling a drug is a violation of the FFDCA, as is the act of introducing or receiving a mislabeled drug in interstate commerce.[29] In order to be properly labeled, prescription drugs must be labeled in accordance with the FDA's extensive labeling requirements.[30] Furthermore, the FFDCA requires that prescription drugs may be dispensed only with a valid prescription.[31] Therefore, it is a violation of the Act to import prescription drugs without a legitimate U.S. prescription.

According to the FDA, a recent inspection of prescription drug shipments by U.S. Customs and Border Patrol found that 1,019 of 1,153 drug shipments from foreign countries violated the FFDCA because they "contained unapproved drugs" that "could pose clear safety problems."[32] Although the reason for the violation varied depending on the shipment, the FDA and CBP found shipments of drugs that, among other things, had never been approved by the FDA, were inadequately labeled (*e.g.*, lacked instructions or were labeled in a foreign language), had been withdrawn from the U.S. market due to safety concerns, could cause dangerous interactions, required monitoring by a doctor, or were controlled substances.[33]

Penalties Under the FFDCA

If a business or consumer violates the FFDCA by importing unapproved or misbranded prescription drugs, there are a number of criminal and civil penalties that may apply. Although the penalties vary depending on the offense, violations of the Act's general prohibitions are a misdemeanor offense punishable by up to a year in prison or a fine of up to $1,000, or both.[34] A violation that occurs after a prior conviction for violating the Act or that is committed with the intent to defraud or mislead is a felony offense punishable by up to three years of imprisonment or up to a $10,000 fine, or both.[35] If a business or consumer knowingly violates the reimportation provision, then the violation is a felony offense punishable by up to 10 years in prison or up to $250,000 in fines.[36] In addition, federal courts are authorized to issue injunctions in order to enjoin violations of the Act.[37]

It is important to note that "[t]hose who aid and abet a criminal violation of the Act, or conspire to violate the Act, can also be found criminally liable."[38] Federal criminal law generally makes it a separate crime to aid or abet any criminal offense against the United States or to conspire to commit a criminal offense against the United States,[39] so illegal importers could potentially be charged with these offenses as well. In addition, the FFDCA explicitly forbids certain acts, as well as the causing of such prohibited acts.[40] Thus, businesses that facilitate the importation of unapproved prescription drugs or the reimportation of U.S.-manufactured prescription drugs may be liable if they are deemed to be "causing" violations of the Act.

Despite the range of penalties that FDA has available to punish those who import prescription drugs in violation of the Act, the agency has clarified that its "highest enforcement priority would not be actions against consumers."[41] Indeed, the FDA exercises its enforcement discretion leniently in this regard by allowing consumers to import certain otherwise illegal prescription drugs under certain circumstances. This enforcement policy, known as the Personal Importation policy, is described in detail below.

The FDA's Personal Importation Policy

Although importing unapproved prescription drugs is a violation of the FFDCA, it is the U.S. Customs and Border Patrol (CBP), not FDA, that has the initial responsibility for examining imported goods at the nation's borders. Accordingly, CBP notifies the FDA if it has detected a mail or baggage shipment of "an FDA-regulated article intended for commercial distribution, an article that FDA has specifically requested be detained, or an FDA regulated article that appears to represent a health fraud or an unknown risk to health."[42] In order to assist agency personnel in determining when to allow or refuse entry to imported drugs, the FDA developed its Personal Importation policy.

Under the FDA's Personal Importation policy, the FDA exercises its enforcement discretion to permit consumers to import otherwise illegal prescription drugs for purposes of personal use. Recognizing that the agency's limited enforcement resources are best directed at commercial shipments of imported drugs rather than personal imports, the FDA may, at its discretion, refrain from taking legal action against illegally imported drugs under the following circumstances:

> a) the intended use is unapproved and for a serious condition for which effective treatment may not be available domestically either through commercial or clinical means; b) there is no known commercialization or promotion to persons residing in the U.S. by those involved in the distribution of the product at issue; c) the product is considered not to represent an unreasonable risk; and d) the individual seeking to import the product affirms in writing that it is for the patient's own use (generally not more than 3 month supply) and provides the name and address of the doctor licensed in the U.S. responsible for his or her treatment with the product, or provides evidence that the product is for the continuation of a treatment begun in a foreign country.[43]

Ultimately, the Personal Importation policy is designed to set forth guidance for agency personnel regarding the FDA's enforcement priorities for imported drugs, but it is not intended to grant a license to consumers to import unapproved prescription drugs into the United States.[44] Indeed, the FDA emphasizes that even if all of the factors above are met, "the drugs remain illegal and FDA may decide that such drugs should be refused entry or seized."[45] Furthermore, this policy does not apply to commercial shipments of unapproved prescription drugs, nor is it intended to permit the importation of foreign versions of drugs that are already approved in the United States. Thus, it appears that personal importations of cheaper versions of prescription drugs that are already available in the U.S. do not conform to the FDA's Personal Importation policy.[46]

Meanwhile, in the recent Medicare Prescription Drug, Improvement, and Modernization Act of 2003, Congress authorized the FDA to allow individuals to import prescription drugs for personal use under certain circumstances.[47] Specifically, the Act requires the Secretary of HHS to allow individuals to import prescription drugs from Canada if the drug:

> (A) is imported from a licensed pharmacy for personal use by an individual, not for resale, in quantities that do not exceed a 90-day supply; (B) is accompanied by a copy of a valid prescription; (C) is imported from Canada, from a seller registered with the Secretary; (D) is a prescription drug approved by the Secretary . . . (E) is in the form of a final finished dosage that was manufactured in [a registered] establishment . . . (F) is imported under such other conditions as the Secretary determines to be necessary to ensure public safety.[48]

Although the new individual importation provisions in the Medicare Act appear similar to the FDA's Personal Importation policy, the legislation contains one important restriction: It stipulates that the new importation provisions will not become effective until and unless the Secretary certifies that the implementation of the provision would "pose no additional risk to the public's health and safety; and [would] result in a significant reduction in the cost of covered products to the American consumer."[49] The current Secretary of HHS, however, has declined to provide such certification in the past, and it is unclear what direction the agency will take in the future. Thus, the new individual importation provisions do not appear to represent a codification of the FDA's Personal Importation policy.

State and Local Importation of Prescription Drugs: Violation of Federal Law?

Just as individual consumers have sought to buy cheaper prescription drugs from foreign sources, several state and local governments are currently considering plans to reimport prescription drugs in order to save money on medicines which they reimburse for or provide to their residents and employees. For example, states such as California, Iowa, Illinois, Minnesota, and New Hampshire have begun exploring the prospect of drug importation, and at least one locality, Springfield, Massachusetts, has already begun to import drugs.[50] Contending that carefully structured state programs will provide a sufficient degree of safety, states argue that they have a duty to explore innovative methods for providing more affordable prescription drugs to their residents, even at the risk of violating federal law.

Each state and local importation plan varies somewhat in the details. Springfield, for example, has been facilitating the purchase of Canadian drugs as part of a plan to provide cheaper medications to city employees, and the city estimates that it has saved it least $750,000 since beginning the program in the summer of 2003.[51] Meanwhile, officials in New Hampshire plan to import prescription drugs from Canada for state prison inmates and certain Medicaid recipients that receive medications through state drug plans. The state also intends to establish a web site for New Hampshire residents to purchase drugs from Canadian pharmacies that are licensed in Canada and approved by the state.[52] In addition, Vermont has petitioned the FDA in hope that the agency will, as it has done with regard to personal drug importation, exercise its enforcement discretion and allow Vermont to provide imported Canadian drugs to state employees.[53]

Despite the efforts of such state and local governments, the FDA continues to maintain that importing unapproved prescription drugs is unsafe and illegal. Indeed, FDA representatives have met with and sought to convince state officials to change their minds about importing drugs in apparent violation of federal law. At the same time, the agency has notified certain states of its legal position regarding drug imports. For example, according to the FDA's response to an inquiry from California officials, "if an entity or person within the State of California (including any state, county, or city program, any public pension, or any Indian Reservation) were to import prescription drugs into the State of California from Canada [or any other foreign country], it would violate FFDCA in virtually every instance."[54]

The FDA provides several legal arguments for reaching its conclusion that state and local drug importation is a violation of the FFDCA. First, the statute prohibits anyone other than the manufacturer from reimporting drugs that were originally manufactured in the United States. Second, even if an FDA-approved drug is manufactured outside the U.S., the imported version of the drug will almost certainly violate statutory requirements regarding drug approvals, labeling, and dispensing.[55] These first two arguments are identical to the arguments that FDA has made when explaining why the agency views business and consumer imports of prescription drugs to be statutory violations.[56] Therefore, the FDA considers virtually any imports of prescription drugs, as well as virtually any act that causes such imports, to be illegal, regardless of whether such imports are conducted by businesses, consumers, or governmental entities.

Finally, the FDA contends that any effort by states to enact legislation authorizing prescription drug imports would be preempted by federal law.[57] Although the FDA sets forth several legal arguments for its position, preemption of the Act's importation provisions does not appear to have been tested in court, and there are several instances in which other prescription drug provisions in the FFDCA have been held not to preempt state law.[58]

Despite the FDA's position regarding state and local imports of prescription drugs, it appears that the agency is currently refraining from taking legal action against state and local governments that are importing such drugs. Although "FDA and industry officials say the agency has not ruled out possible future legal action," "the agency wants to first win its case against Rx Depot, giving FDA bargaining power for the more difficult task of taking formal action against states and local governments."[59] In the Rx Depot case, which is discussed in detail in the following section, the FDA is pursuing legal action against a private company that helps individual consumers import prescription drugs.

Businesses That Facilitate Importation of Prescription Drugs

As noted above, the FDA is currently refraining from taking legal action against both states and individual consumers who import prescription drugs in violation of the FFDCA because the agency has instead chosen to focus its initial enforcement effort on pursuing businesses that facilitate the importation of such drugs. Unlike pharmacies, which receive orders from consumers and dispense drugs directly, some businesses facilitate drug sales without dispensing drugs directly. Rather, these companies, many of which are online, act as middlemen between consumers, who provide medical and payment information, and foreign (typically Canadian) pharmacies, which then ship drugs directly to consumers. The FDA is currently pursuing legal action against one such business. That case is discussed in detail in this section, while separate but related issues involving online pharmacies are discussed in a separate section below.

In *United States v. Rx Depot*,[60] the Department of Justice (DOJ), acting on behalf of the FDA, filed suit against Rx Depot, a storefront operation that helps U.S. consumers obtain prescription drugs from Canada.[61] According to the suit, DOJ contends that Rx Depot is violating two provisions of the FFDCA, namely the provision prohibiting reimportation and the provision prohibiting the introduction into interstate commerce of any drug that violates the Act's approval requirements.[62] Although Rx Depot is not directly importing drugs, the company admits that it is "engaged in the business of causing the shipment of U.S.-manufactured and unapproved, foreign-manufactured prescription drugs from Canadian pharmacies to U.S. citizens."[63]

Rx Depot has countered that the FDA is not actually concerned about the safety of imported drugs because the agency never tested the drugs it bought from Rx Depot as part of a sting operation against the company.[64] Similar complaints have been voiced by other businesses that facilitate the importation of prescription drugs. Critics of FDA's importation stance also argue that it "fails to protect the public health because it allows individuals to import drugs, while prohibiting 'commercial' operations that are in the best position to develop safeguards,"[65] and allege that the FDA's importation policy may violate international trade agreements.[66] Ultimately, critics argue that the FDA's policy protects the profits of drug manufacturers at the expense of consumer pocketbooks.[67]

Despite these arguments, the district court held against Rx Depot during a preliminary ruling in the case. Concluding that "Rx Depot's importation of prescription drugs clearly violates the law," the district court issued a preliminary injunction enjoining Rx Depot from facilitating the importation of prescription drugs.[68] While the court's order is not actually a final order on the merits of the case, it does indicate that DOJ has a substantial likelihood of prevailing in the lawsuit. Indeed, the court appeared particularly concerned with the safety of imported drugs:

> [U]napproved prescription drugs and drugs imported from foreign countries by someone other than the U.S.-manufacturer do not have the same assurance of safety and efficacy as drugs regulated by the Food and Drug Administration... Because the drugs are not subject to FDA oversight and are not continuously under the custody of a U.S. manufacturer or authorized distributor, their quality is less predictable than drugs obtained in the United States. For instance, the drugs may be contaminated, counterfeit, or contain erratic amounts of the active ingredient or different excipients. Also, the drugs may have been held under uncertain storage conditions, and therefore be outdated or subpotent.[69]

With regard to Rx Depot, the court specifically noted that drugs ordered through the company were often dispensed in quantities greater than prescribed and did not contain the required package inserts. Although the court acknowledged that the cost of prescription drugs in the U.S. is high and that there are no known cases of an individual who has suffered harm from drugs imported through Rx Depot, the court nevertheless concluded that the FDA has legitimate safety concerns and that Congress is in the best position to resolve the tension between prescription drug safety and cost.[70]

As noted above, the district court's decision to issue a preliminary injunction against Rx Depot is not a final decision on the merits of the case. Meanwhile, as the legal battle continues, many companies like Rx Depot remain in business, and an increasing number of states and localities have begun to contemplate their own importation programs. In response, several drug manufacturers have begun limiting sales of their drugs to Canadian pharmacies in an effort to prevent the drugs from being resold in the U.S. at cheaper prices. These actions have raised questions about whether such behavior violates federal antitrust laws, a topic that is discussed in the following section.

Antitrust Laws

As noted above, several major prescription drug manufacturers have responded to the rise in the number of businesses and consumers that are reimporting cheaper drugs into the U.S. by reducing the supply of such drugs to distributors and pharmacies in Canada, where most of the reimported drugs originate. Such moves appear to be intended to limit Canadian distributors and pharmacies to selling prescription drugs to Canadian consumers only, rather than selling excess supplies of prescription drugs to U.S. consumers at cheaper prices than such consumers would pay for similar drugs in the U.S. As a result, several members of Congress have questioned whether these drug manufacturers are violating federal antitrust laws,[71] and several bills introduced in the 108th Congress would prohibit such sales tactics.[72] In addition, at least one state has launched an investigation into whether or not the drug manufacturer GlaxoSmithKline (GSK) has violated state antitrust laws.[73] This section discusses the potential federal and state antitrust issues raised by the decision of certain drug manufacturers to limit the supply of drugs to Canadian distributors and pharmacies.

Federal Antitrust Law

Under federal law, the Sherman Act,[74] one of the major federal antitrust statutes, makes illegal "[e]very contract, combination in the form of trust or otherwise, or conspiracy, in restraint of trade or commerce . . ."[75] The statute does not, however, prohibit independent action by a single entity; the Supreme Court has specifically stated:

The Sherman Act contains a 'basic distinction between concerted and independent action.' The conduct of a single firm is governed by § 2 alone and is unlawful only when it threatens actual monopolization. . . . Section 1 of the Sherman Act, in contrast, reaches unreasonable restraints of trade effected by a 'contract, combination . . . or conspiracy between *separate* entities. It does not reach conduct that is wholly unilateral.'[76]

Nevertheless, a formal contract may not be necessary to show collective action that violates section 1 of the Sherman Act.[77] To define how much proof is necessary to find an "inference of agreement"[78] a number of cases have examined the question of what constitutes the establishment of collective action. For example, *American Tobacco Co. v. United States*,[79] an early Supreme Court case in this area, defined agreement as "a unity of purpose or a common design and understanding or a meeting of minds in an unlawful arrangement."[80] Later decisions have reasoned that these agreements may be found even without verbal statements among the parties.[81] In *Monsanto Co. v. Spray-Rite Service Corp.*,[82] the Supreme Court established a standard for determining whether concerted action exists:

The correct standard is that there must be evidence that tends to exclude the possibility of independent action by the [parties]. That is, there must be direct or circumstantial evidence that reasonably tends to prove that [the parties] had a conscious commitment to a common scheme designed to achieve an unlawful objective.[83]

Courts often use the term "conscious parallelism" or "consciously parallel behavior" to refer to actions by competitors that are based on a pattern of uniform business conduct. In the early case *Interstate Circuit, Inc. v. United States*,[84] the Supreme Court held that the nearly identical restraints imposed by eight motion picture distributors concerning the licensing of first run "feature" pictures was sufficient to infer that the distributors acted in concert and thereby violated the federal antitrust laws.

It is elementary that an unlawful conspiracy may be and often is formed without simultaneous action or agreement on the part of the conspirators. Acceptance by competitors, without previous agreement, of an invitation to participate in a plan, the necessary consequence of which, if carried out, is restraint of interstate commerce, is sufficient to establish an unlawful conspiracy under the Sherman Act.[85]

However, in *Theatre Enterprises v. Paramount Film Distributing Corp.*,[86] the Supreme Court held that parallel behavior by itself is not necessarily proof of a conspiracy. The Court stated:

The crucial question is whether respondents' conduct toward petitioner stemmed from independent decision or from an agreement, tacit or express. To be sure, business behavior is admissible circumstantial evidence from which the fact finder may find agreement. But this Court has never held that proof of parallel business behavior conclusively establishes agreement or, phrased differently, that such behavior itself constitutes a Sherman Act offense. Circumstantial evidence of consciously parallel behavior may have made heavy inroads into the traditional judicial attitude toward conspiracy; but "conscious parallelism" has not yet read conspiracy out of the Sherman Act entirely.[87]

Lower courts, in following these Supreme Court decisions, have seemed for the most part to hold that conscious parallelism by itself does not show that the parties have violated the Sherman Act.[88] The courts have required that other factors be looked at in conjunction with parallel behavior to find concerted action resulting in a Sherman Act violation. Some of these other factors include artificial standardization of products[89] and raising prices in time of surplus.[90] Less persuasive is evidence that indicates merely that the parties had an opportunity to collude.[91]

Based upon these cases and assuming that there is no evidence that the drug manufacturers in question conspired or colluded when reducing drug supplies to Canadian distributors and pharmacies, it would appear difficult to sustain a charge that the drug companies that limit sales to Canada have violated the Sherman Act. Indeed, there may be lawful reasons for their actions. For example, the manufacturers may be capable of supplying only the United States market and to a lesser extent foreign markets because of limited production capacity. They may also need to recoup research and development costs by obtaining a profit margin through sales primarily in the U.S. However, if one were able to show that the drug companies did in fact conspire or collude or that they engaged in parallel behavior accompanied by other factors, a case might be made for a Sherman Act violation.

Despite the apparent lack of violation of federal antitrust law, drug manufacturers that limit sales of prescription drugs to Canadian distributors and pharmacies may still violate state antitrust laws. Because antitrust laws vary from state to state, this section does not provide an exhaustive analysis of state antitrust laws, but rather describes the current legal dispute against GlaxoSmithKline (GSK) in Minnesota as an example of potential liability under state antitrust statutes.

State Antitrust Law

Although most states have their own antitrust laws, enforcement of these statutes differs from state to state. In October 2003, the Minnesota Attorney General (AG), who is investigating whether GSK violated state antitrust laws, filed a court motion seeking to compel GSK to release information about the company's decision to stop selling drugs to Canadian pharmacies that then sell the drugs to U.S. consumers. According to the AG, GSK conspired to limit drug sales to Canada, and "GSK's refusal to supply prescription drugs to Canadian pharmacies that sell drugs to Minnesota buyers violates state laws."[92] Meanwhile, GSK contends that "importing drugs from Canada is illegal and a drug company can take steps to stop illegal sales of its products."[93] The company further argues that federal law preempts Minnesota's antitrust laws, but the Minnesota AG challenges that assertion. Although no lawsuit has actually been filed against GSK, the Minnesota AG may decide to file such a suit if the court grants its motion to compel GSK's release of documents and if the AG subsequently finds evidence of an antitrust violation.[94]

III. INTERNET PHARMACIES

Just as the FDA has expressed concerns about the safety of imported drugs, federal regulators have become increasingly worried about the safety of online pharmacies and prescription drug sales over the Internet. Indeed, the regulation of prescription drug importation and the regulation of online pharmacies often overlap because many consumers use online pharmacies to purchase imported drugs. Regardless of whether or not drugs purchased online are imported, the FDA is worried about the safety of such medications because of concerns about the lack of adequate physician supervision for consumers who purchase prescription drugs online, the prospects for tampering with or counterfeiting such drugs, and the possibility that such drugs may be handled, dispensed, packaged, or shipped incorrectly. This section discusses current laws and regulations that govern online pharmacies and physicians who prescribe medications over the Internet. Specifically, this section provides an overview of the various federal and state laws that regulate this field, including laws covering prescription drugs, controlled substances, pharmacies, and the practice of medicine.

With the advent of the Internet, many individuals have turned from traditional neighborhood to large chains with a neighborhood presence and online pharmacies to purchase prescription drugs, and an increasing number of physicians have incorporated the Internet and email into their medical practice. Use of this technology has many advantages for both the doctor and the patient, including cost savings, convenience, accessibility, and improved privacy and communication.[95] Although many online pharmacies are legitimate businesses that offer safe and convenient services similar to those provided by traditional neighborhood pharmacies, other online pharmacies – often referred to as "rogue sites" – engage in practices that are illegal, such as selling unapproved or counterfeit drugs or dispensing drugs without a prescription.[96] Some rogue sites operate in a legal gray area in which the online pharmacy, as mandated by federal law, requires a prescription before dispensing prescription drugs, but allows patients to secure a prescription by completing an online questionnaire that is reviewed by a doctor who never examines or speaks to the patient. This practice, though potentially unsafe for patients who may be diagnosed incorrectly, is not necessarily illegal.

Current regulation of online pharmacies and doctors consists of a patchwork of federal and state laws in an array of areas. At the federal level, the FDA regulates prescription drugs under the FFDCA, which governs, among other things, the safety and efficacy of prescription medications, including the approval, manufacturing, and distribution of such drugs.[97] It is the FFDCA that requires that prescription drugs may be dispensed only with a valid prescription.[98] The DEA enforces the Controlled Substances Act (CSA), which is a federal statute that establishes criminal and civil sanctions for the unlawful possession, manufacturing, or distribution of certain addictive or dangerous substances, including certain prescription drugs that share these properties, such as narcotics and opiates.[99] At the state level, state boards of pharmacy regulate pharmacy practice, and state medical boards oversee the practice of medicine.[100] Thus, some of the laws that govern online pharmacies and doctors vary from state to state. The laws that govern each of these areas are described separately below.

Federal Oversight

As noted above, the CSA is a federal statute that establishes criminal and civil sanctions for the unlawful possession, manufacturing, or distribution of addictive or dangerous substances.[101] Although the CSA is generally known for prohibiting illegal drugs like heroin and cocaine and does not include many drugs legally available by prescription, the statute does cover certain prescription drugs that have addictive properties, such as narcotics and opiates that are often used in the treatment of pain.

It is the latter category of prescription painkillers that appear to be among the drugs most heavily dispensed by certain Internet pharmacies in accordance with prescriptions that are issued based on online questionnaires.[102] This practice has sometimes been abused by rogue sites that dispense large quantities of addictive substances to customers apparently seeking access to prescription painkillers, and it has lead to instances of addiction, overdose, and death. In response to cases in which online doctors have written thousands of prescriptions for controlled substances without examining their patients, the federal government has begun prosecuting certain doctors under the CSA by charging them with the illegal distribution of controlled substances.[103] Penalties under the CSA vary depending on the amount and type of substance involved but generally include monetary fines, forfeiture, and imprisonment.[104]

As noted above, prescription drugs are also regulated by the FDA under the FFDCA.[105] Although state law also governs the prescribing of drugs, the FFDCA covers certain aspects of the prescribing process, including the requirement that prescription drugs may not be dispensed without a valid prescription.[106]

Although federal law requires that prescription drugs be dispensed in accordance with a prescription, the FFDCA does not define the meaning of "prescription." Rather, each state defines what constitutes a valid prescription under its pharmacy laws. Because such definitions differ from state to state, there is no uniform, national definition of the term "prescription."[107] Thus, certain activities, such as prescribing drugs without performing an in-person examination, may be explicitly illegal in one state but of ambiguous legal status in another.

Concerned about reports of rogue online pharmacies, Congress has considered legislation to establish a federal definition of what constitutes a valid prescription.[108] During the Clinton Administration, for example, legislators contemplated requiring online pharmacies to disclose information about themselves and about the doctors approving prescriptions on their sites, but the legislation ultimately faded.[109] In the wake of recent reports of abuses by online pharmacies, however, interest in such legislation has revived, and Congress recently held hearings to discuss legislative solutions, including the establishment of a single federal standard for prescriptions.[110]

Congress is also exploring the possibility of controlling the means by which allegedly rogue sites do business, namely by restricting their ability to advertise on search engines, make credit card sales, and ship prescription drugs to consumers. For example, Google, an Internet search engine, recently announced that it no longer accepts advertising from unlicenced pharmacies and now prohibits the use of certain controlled substances as keywords for search purposes.[111] Meanwhile, at least three congressional committees are investigating "the roles played by Visa International, MasterCard Inc., FedEx Corp. and United Parcel Service Inc. in the Internet sales,"[112] as well as exploring the prospects for establishing a certification program that would make it easy for such companies to determine when they are doing business with a legitimate site.[113] Because federal and state regulators face many legal barriers when attempting to exercise jurisdiction over rogue pharmacies based in foreign countries,[114] placing limits on the degree to which search engines, credit card companies, and shipping entities facilitate prescription drug purchases from rogue sites may be one of the only ways to control illicit sales by foreign online pharmacies.

State Oversight

As noted above, state boards of pharmacy are primarily responsible for regulating pharmacy practice,[115] although the FFDCA does provide some federal oversight of pharmacies. Because virtually all states require a pharmacy that sells drugs in the state to be licensed with the state, a state board of pharmacy traditionally may exercise regulatory authority over pharmacies and pharmacists located within the state, as well as those that dispense medication across state lines to citizens within the state.[116]

Because each state board of pharmacy sets its own policies with regard to both online and traditional pharmacies, state pharmacy laws regarding Internet pharmacies and doctors differ from state to state. While some state laws specify whether or not prescriptions based on online questionnaires are valid, other state laws fail to address the issue, thus rendering it difficult for some states to prosecute doctors who prescribe drugs without performing an in-person evaluation. For this reason, some critics of the current system have proposed establishing a federal definition of what constitutes a valid prescription.[117]

In addition, some organizations have begun to promote uniform national standards for the industry. For example, the National Association of Boards of Pharmacy (NABP), whose members include all 50 state boards, is an organization that helps state boards of pharmacy by developing uniform standards on pharmacy practice. In response to the proliferation of online pharmacies, NABP established the Verified Internet Pharmacy Practice Sites (VIPPS) program, a certification program that "identifies to the public those online pharmacy practice sites that are appropriately licensed, are legitimately operating via the Internet, and that have successfully completed a rigorous criteria review and inspection."[118]

According to NABP, the VIPPS program was developed in order to improve the safety of online pharmacy practices and to "provide a means for the public to distinguish between legitimate and illegitimate online pharmacy practice sites."[119] Although NABP notes that legitimate online pharmacies outnumber rogue sites and acknowledges that there are many advantages to ordering drugs online, the Association specifically warns consumers against buying prescription drugs online without obtaining an in-person examination and valid prescription from a doctor.

Like pharmacy practice, the practice of medicine has historically been regulated at the state level by state medical boards. According to the Federation of State Medical Boards (FSMB), which coordinates policy among all 50 state medical boards, "[t]he primary responsibility and obligation of a state medical board is to protect consumers of health care through proper licensing and regulation of physicians."[120] Traditionally, states enact laws that regulate the practice of medicine, and state medical boards implement and oversee state policies.[121] If a doctor violates a state law or regulation, state medical boards generally have the authority to discipline the doctor through modification, suspension, or revocation of the doctor's license to practice medicine in that state. In reality, however, laws regarding medical practice vary widely in strength and effectiveness from state to state. While some states have strong laws that explicitly prohibit activities such as prescribing drugs without conducting an in-person examination, other states have weak laws, lax enforcement, or both.

Like NABP, FSMB has developed a specific policy with regard to online pharmacies and doctors that prescribe drugs over the Internet. According to FSMB's model guidelines on the subject, electronic technology "should supplement and enhance, but not replace, crucial interpersonal interactions that create the very basis of the physician-patient relationship."[122] To that end, FSMB guidelines declare that doctors who use the Internet as part of their medical practice should conduct a physical evaluation of the patient before providing treatment. Although FSMB recognizes the benefits of online pharmacies, the organization emphasizes that "[t]reatment, including issuing a prescription, based solely on an online questionnaire or consultation does not constitute an acceptable standard of care."[123] FSMB further urges that doctors who prescribe drugs on the Internet should be licensed in all states in which their patients reside,[124] a practice that would subject doctors to the oversight of the medical boards in each state in which their patients lived.[125] These professional standards, however, are not legally enforceable in the absence of state laws establishing such requirements.

IV. CONCLUSION

The current legal framework for regulating online pharmacies and doctors is a patchwork of federal and state laws regarding controlled substances, prescription drugs, pharmacies, and the practice of medicine. Although many doctors and pharmacies who use the Internet prescribe and dispense drugs in a responsible, safe, and legal fashion, others have exploited gaps in the current system to prescribe and dispense potentially dangerous quantities of highly addictive prescription drugs. To combat such abuses, legislators and interest groups have proposed an array of solutions, including establishing a federal definition of what constitutes a valid prescription, requiring doctors to conduct in-person examinations, mandating that online pharmacies disclose identifying information about themselves and the doctors who work for them, giving state prosecutors the authority to seek nationwide injunctions against rogue sites, educating consumers about the potential dangers of buying drugs online, and establishing certification programs to identify legitimate online pharmacies.

Meanwhile, the debate about importing prescription drugs continues as well. Although the FDA maintains that it cannot guarantee the safety of imported drugs, many U.S. consumers, in search of affordable prices, continue to purchase such drugs in increasing numbers. As a result, legislators and interest groups have suggested a variety of changes to current law, including encouraging the development of more generic drugs, negotiating lower drug prices through bulk purchase programs, increasing prescription drug insurance coverage, allowing drug imports but restricting ports of entry, educating consumers about the dangers of imported drugs, and allowing drug imports from approved Canadian pharmacies only

REFERENCES

[1] Pub. L. No. 108-173 [hereinafter Medicare Act]. The original certification provision was contained in the Medicine Equity and Drug Safety (MEDS) Act. Pub. L. No. 106-387.

[2] The Canadian government has also stated that it cannot guarantee the safety of drugs exported to the U.S. from Canada. Marc Kaufman, *Canadian Drug Position Misinterpreted*, Wash. Post, May 26, 2003, at A11.

[3] Marc Kaufman, *FDA's Authority Tested Over Drug Imports*, Wash. Post, Nov. 9, 2003, at A11.

[4] *Id.*

[5] *Id.*

[6] Inside Washington Publishers, *Canadians Pay More for Drugs When Per Capita Income Adjusted*, FDA Week, Dec. 19, 2003, at 1.

[7] Gardiner Harris, *The Nation: Prescriptions Filled; If Americans Want to Pay Less for Drugs, They Will*, N.Y. Times, Nov. 16, 2003, § 4, at 4.

[8] Food and Drug Administration, *Buying Medicines and Medical Products Online*, http://www.fda.gov/oc/buyonline/default.htm.

[9] [For other information on prescription drug importation and Internet sales, see CRS Report RL31503, *Importing Prescription Drugs*; CRS Report RL32107, *Importing Prescription Drugs – Comparison of the Drug Import Provisions in the Medicare Reform Bills, H.R. 2427, and Current Law*; and GAO Report GAO-01-69, *Internet Pharmacies: Adding Disclosure Requirements Would Aid State and Federal Oversight*.

[10] 21 U.S.C. § 301 et seq.

[11] *Id.* at § 353(b).
[12] *Id.* at § 801 et seq. For more information on the Controlled Substances Act, see CRS Report 97-141A, *Drug Smuggling, Drug Dealing and Drug Abuse: Background and Overview of the Sanctions Under the Federal Controlled Substances Act and Related Statutes.*
[13] 21 U.S.C. § 301 et seq.
[14] *Id.* at § 381(d)(1). The Secretary, however, is authorized to allow the importation of any drugs that are required for emergency medical care. *Id.* at § 381(d)(2).
[15] Under the FDA's Personal Importation policy, however, the FDA currently does not enforce this prohibition against individuals who import a limited supply of prescription drugs for personal use. *See infra* notes 42-49 and accompanying text.
[16] Letter from William K. Hubbard, Associate Commissioner for Policy and Planning, Food and Drug Administration, to Robert P. Lombardi, Esq., The Kullman Firm 1 (Feb. 12, 2003), http://www.fda.gov/ora/import/kullman.pdf [hereinafter Lombardi Letter].
[17] Pub. L. No. 106-387.
[18] 21 U.S.C. § 384.
[19] *Id.* at § 384(l).
[20] Medicare Act, *supra* note 1.
[21] *Id.*
[22] *Id.* This legislation, which is similar to the FDA's Personal Importation policy, is discussed in more detail in a separate section below.
[23] *Id.*
[24] Lombardi Letter, *supra* note 16 at 2.
[25] 21 U.S.C. § 355.
[26] *Id.* at § 353(b)(2).
[27] *Id.* at § 353(b)(1).
[28] Lombardi Letter, *supra* note 16 at 3.
[29] 21 U.S.C. §§ 331 (a)-(c), 353(b)(2).
[30] 21 C.F.R. §201.100(c)(2).
[31] 21 U.S.C. § 353(b)(1).
[32] Press Release, Food and Drug Administration, FDA/U.S. Customs Import Blitz Exams Reveal Hundreds of Potentially Dangerous Imported Drug Shipments (Sept. 29, 2003), http://www.fda.gov/bbs/topics/NEWS/2003/NEW00948.html.
[33] *Id.*

[34] 21 U.S.C. § 333(a)(1). In addition, misdemeanor violations of the Act are strict liability offenses. United States v. Dotterweich, 320 U.S. 277, 284 (1943).
[35] 21 U.S.C. § 333(a)(2).
[36] *Id.* at §§ 333(b)(1), 381(d)(1).
[37] *Id.* at § 332.
[38] Lombardi Letter, *supra* note 16 at 1.
[39] 18 U.S.C. §§ 2, 371.
[40] 21 U.S.C. § 331.
[41] Lombardi Letter, *supra* note 16 at 4.
[42] Office of Regulatory Affairs, Food and Drug Administration, *Coverage of Personal Importations*, R Egulatory P Rocedures M Anual, http://www.fda.gov/ora/ compliance_ref/rpm_new2/ch9pers.html.
[43] *Id. See also*, Office of Regulatory Affairs, Food and Drug Administration, *Importation of Prescription Medicines/ Drugs*, http://www.fda.gov/ora/import/traveler_alert.htm; Office of Regulatory Affairs, Food and Drug Administration, *Information on Importation of Drugs* (April 3, 1998), http://www.fda.gov/ora/import/pipinfo.htm.
[44] Office of Regulatory Affairs, Food and Drug Administration, *Coverage of Personal Importations*, R Egulatory P Rocedures M Anual, http://www.fda.gov/ora/compliance_ref/rpm_new2/ch9pers.html.
[45] Office of Regulatory Affairs, Food and Drug Administration, *Importation of Prescription Medicines/Drugs*, http://www.fda.gov/ora/import/traveler_alert.htm.
[46] Office of Regulatory Affairs, Food and Drug Administration, *Information on Importation of Drugs* (April 3, 1998), http://www.fda.gov/ora/import/pipinfo.htm.
[47] Medicare Act, *supra* note 1 at § 1121.
[48] *Id.*
[49] *Id.*
[50] Pam Belluck, *Boldly Crossing the Line for Cheaper Drugs*, N. Y. Times, Dec. 11, 2003, (continued...) at A38.
[51] *Id.*
[52] *Id.*
[53] Inside Washington Publishers, *Vermont Wants FDA to Allow Drug Reimportation for State Employees*, FDA WEEK, Dec. 19, 2003, at 3. The new Medicare bill authorizes the FDA to provide waivers for

individual importation, and some lawmakers are arguing that the individual importation waiver authority extends to state importation plans because such plans are intended to provide prescription drugs to individual state residents. The FDA, however, notes that the waiver provisions in the Medicare bill become effective only upon certification by the Secretary that drug importation is safe and reduces costs. Kelly Field, *Battle Brewing Between Administration, Local Officials Over Drug Importation Issue*, CQ TODAY, Dec. 19, 2003.

[54] Letter from William K. Hubbard, Associate Commissioner for Policy and Planning, Food and Drug Administration, to Gregory Gonot, Deputy Attorney General, State of California 2 (Aug. 25, 2003), http://www.fda.gov/opacom/gonot.html [hereinafter California Letter].

[55] *Id.* at 3.

[56] See *supra* notes 14-33 and accompanying text.

[57] California Letter, *supra* note 54 at 5-7. The preemption doctrine derives from the Supremacy Clause of the Constitution, which establishes that the laws of the United States "shall be the supreme law of the land; and the judges in every state shall be bound thereby, any thing in the Constitution or laws of any State to the contrary notwithstanding." U.S. CONST. art. VI, cl. 2. In applying this constitutional mandate, courts have recognized both express and implied forms of preemption, which are "compelled whether Congress' command is explicitly stated in the statute's language, or implicitly contained in its structure and purpose." Gade v. National Solid Wastes Management Association, 505 U.S. 88, 97 (1992) (quoting Jones v. Rath Packing Co., 430 U.S. 519, 525 (1977)).

[58] Many of these cases, however, deal with prescription drug labeling, not importation, and state common law claims, not state statutory law. David R. Geiger and Mark D. Rosen, *Rationalizing Product Liability for Prescription Drugs: Implied Preemption, Federal Common Law, and Other Paths to Uniform Pharmaceutical Safety Standards*, 45 Depaul L. REV. 395, 408 (1996). It is also important to note that the FFDCA expressly preempts state law with regard to over-the-counter drugs and medical devices but not with regard to prescription drugs. As a result, it is more difficult to predict the outcome of a preemption challenge to state laws on prescription drugs. A detailed examination of the preemption issue, however, is beyond the scope of this article.

[59] Inside Washington Publishers, *FDA To Resolve Rx Depot Suit Before Taking on States,* FDA Week, Oct. 31, 2003, at 1, 1, 8.

[60] No. 03-CV-0616-EA (M), 2003 U.S. Dist. LEXIS 20135 (D. Okla. Nov. 6) (order granting preliminary injunction).
[61] DOJ initiated this lawsuit after Rx Depot failed to respond to the agency's warning letter and continued to facilitate the reimportation of prescription drugs and the importation of unapproved drugs. *See* Letter from David J. Horowitz, Esq., Director, Office of Compliance, Center for Drug Evaluation and Research, Food and Drug Administration, to Harry Lee Jones, Store Manager, Rx Depot, Inc., (March 21, 2003), http://www.fda.gov/foi/warning_letters/g3888d.htm. FDA has sent similar warning letters to other businesses that facilitate the importation of prescription drugs. *See, e.g.*, Letter from David J. Horowitz, Esq., Director, Office of Compliance, Center for Drug Evaluation and Research, Food and Drug Administration, to G. Anthony Howard, President, CanaRx Services, Inc., (Sept. 16, 2003), http://www.fda.gov/cder/warn/2003/RHoward.pdf. CanaRx is the business that currently assists Springfield, Massachusetts in importing prescription drugs. Press Release, Food and Drug Administration, CanaRx Illegally Supplying Prescription Drugs (Nov .6, 2003), http://www.fda.gov/bbs/topics/NEWS/2003/NEW00973.html.
[62] [*United States v. Rx Depot*, 2003 U.S. Dist. LEXIS 20135 (D. Okla. Nov. 6) (order granting preliminary injunction). *See also*, 21 U.S.C. §§ 331(d), 331(t), and 355.
[63] *Id.* at *6-*7.
[64] Inside Washington Publishers, *Rx Depot: FDA Alleged Safety Concerns With Reimportation Are Bogus*, FDA Week, Nov. 7, 2003, at 15.
[65] *Id.* at 16.
[66] Inside Washington Publishers, *CanaRx Says FDA's Reimportation Policy Violates Trade Agreements*, FDA Week, Nov. 7, 2003, at 16. An analysis of international trade agreements is beyond the scope of this report.
[67] Marc Kaufman, *FDA's Authority Tested Over Drug Imports*, Wash. Post, Nov. 9, 2003, at A11.
[68] *United States v. Rx Depot*, 2003 U.S. Dist. LEXIS at *23, *36.
[69] *Id.* at *8.
[70] *Id.* at *8-*9, *16-*18.
[71] Inside Washington Publishers, *Lawmakers Seek DOJ Anti-Trust Probe of Firms Limiting Sales to Canada*, FDA Week, Nov. 7, 2003, at 3.
[72] *See, e.g.*, H.R. 2497, H.R. 2769, S. 1992.

[73] Inside Washington Publishers, *Judge Wants More Info Before Deciding Motion to Compel Against GSK*, FDA Week, Nov. 21, 2003, at 10.
[74] 15 U.S.C. §§ 1-7.
[75] 15 U.S.C. § 1.
[76] *Copperweld Corp. v. Independence Tube Corp.*, 467 U.S. 752, 767-68 (1984)(citations and footnote omitted).
[77] *See, e.g., United States v. General Motors Corp.*, 384 U.S. 127, 142-43 (1966) (stating "it has long been settled that explicit agreement is not a necessary part of a Sherman Act conspiracy").
[78] ABA Section of Antitrust Law, Antitrust Law Developments 4 (4th ed. 1997).
[79] 328 U.S. 781 (1946).
[80] *Id.* at 810.
[81] *See e.g., United States v. General Motors Corp.*, 384 U.S. 127, 142-43 (1966) (stating that "although we regard as clearly erroneous and irreconcilable with its other findings the trial court's conclusory 'finding' that there had been no 'agreement' among the defendants and their alleged co-conspirators, it has long been settled that explicit agreement is not a necessary part of a Sherman Act conspiracy—certainly not where, as here, joint and collaborative action was pervasive in the initiation, execution, and fulfillment of the plan").
[82] 465 U.S. 752 (1984).
[83] *Id.* at 768.
[84] 306 U.S. 208 (1939).
[85] *Id.* at 227 (citations omitted).
[86] 346 U.S. 537 (1954).
[87] *Id.* at 540-41 (citations omitted).
[88] *See, e.g., Wallace v. Bank of Bartlett*, 55 F.3d 1166, 1168 (6th Cir. 1995), *cert. denied* 116 S.Ct. 709 1996) (stating that "parallel pricing, without more, does not itself establish a violation. . . . Courts require additional evidence which they have described as 'plus factors'"). *See also, Todorov v. DCH Healthcare Auth.*, 921 F.2d 1438, 1456 (11th Cir. 1990) (stating that "we require more than mere evidence of parallel conduct by competitors to support an inference of a conspiracy").
[89] *C-O-Two Fire Equip. Co. v. United States*, 197 F.2d 489 (9th Cir. 1952), *cert. denied*, 344 U.S. 892 (1952).
[90] *American Tobacco Co. v. United States*, 328 U.S. 781 (1946).

[91] *See, e.g., Greater Rockford Energy & Tech. Corp. v. Shell Oil Co.*, 998 F.2d 391 (7th Cir. 1993).
[92] Inside Washington Publishers, *Judge Wants More Info Before Deciding Motion to Compel Against GSK*, FDA Week, Nov. 21, 2003, at 10, 10.
[93] *Id.*
[94] *Id.*
[95] Food and Drug Administration, U.S. Department of Agriculture, *Buying Drugs Online: It's Convenient and Private, But Beware of 'Rogue Sites'* (2001), *at* http://www.fda.gov/fdac/features/2000/100_online.html.
[96] [*Id.*
[97] 21 U.S.C. § 301 et seq.
[98] *Id.* at § 353(b).
[99] *Id.* at § 801 et seq. For more information on the Controlled Substances Act, see CRS Report 97-141A, *Drug Smuggling, Drug Dealing and Drug Abuse: Background and Overview of the Sanctions Under the Federal Controlled Substances Act and Related Statutes*.
[100] The FFDCA excludes the practice of medicine from its jurisdiction. 21 U.S.C. § 396.
[101] *Id.* at § 801 et seq.
[102] *See, e.g.*, Gilbert M. Gaul and Mary Pat Flaherty, *Doctors Medicate Strangers on Web*, Wash. Post, Oct. 21, 2003, at A1.
[103] *Id.*
[104] [21 U.S.C. § 841 et seq.
[105] *Id* at § 301 et seq.
[106] *Id.* at § 353(b).
[107] Inside Washington Publishers, *FDA May Back Changing Law to Define Internet 'Prescription'*, FDA Week, March 28, 2003, *at* 1, 10.
[108] *Id.* at 1.
[109] Gilbert M. Gaul and Mary Pat Flaherty, *Doctors Medicate Strangers on Web*, WASH. POST, Oct. 21, 2003, at A1.
[110] *Point, Click, Self-Medicate: A Review of Consumer Safeguards on Internet Pharmacy Sites: Hearing Before the House Comm. On Government Reform*, 108th Cong. (2003), http://reform.house.gov/UploadedFiles/Online%20Pharmacies%20Final%20Print.pdf.
[111] Gilbert M. Gaul and Mary Pat Flaherty, *Google to Limit Some Drug Ads*, Wash. Post, Dec. 1, 2003, at A1.
[112] *Id.*

[113] Inside Washington Publishers, *FDA Rep: Internet Pharmacy Certification Could Be Easy Process*, FDA Week, Dec. 19, 2003, at 5.
[114] "The enforcement of a state action or the initiation of a mutual action by a foreign licensing body is virtually unheard of, making it difficult, if not impossible, for state actions to have any effect on foreign pharmacies." National Association of Boards of Pharmacy, *Position Paper on the Importation of Foreign Prescription Drugs* 6 (March 2003), at http://www.nabp.net.
[115] National Association of Boards of Pharmacy, *Verified Internet Pharmacy Practice Sites (VIPPS): Most Frequently Asked Questions* (2001), at http://www.nabp.net.
[116] *Id.* "These requirements allow state boards of pharmacy to order non-resident pharmacies to stop shipping product into the state. Within the US, such orders can be enforced by the board of pharmacy where the violation took place, or by mutual action by the board of pharmacy in the state where the pharmacy is located." National Association of Boards of Pharmacy, *Position Paper on the Importation of Foreign Prescription Drugs* 6 (March 2003), at http://www.nabp.net. Foreign shipments of prescription drugs may also violate state laws if the foreign pharmacy is not licensed in the state, although states often face legal barriers when attempting to exercise jurisdiction over foreign pharmacies.
[117] Inside Washington Publishers, *FDA May Back Changing Law to Define Internet 'Prescription'*, FDA Week, March 28, 2003, *at* 1, 1. *See also, supra* notes 107-10 and accompanying text.
[118] National Association of Boards of Pharmacy, *Verified Internet Pharmacy Practice Sites (VIPPS): Most Frequently Asked Questions* (2001), at http://www.nabp.net.
[119] *Id.*
[120] Federation of State Medical Boards, *What is a State Medical Board?*, *at* http://www.fsmb.org.
[121] *Id.*
[122] *Id.*
[123] Federation of State Medical Boards, *Model Guidelines for the Appropriate Use of the Internet in Medical Practice* (2002), *at* http://www.fsmb.org.
[124] *Id.*
[125] FSMB is not the only medical organization to promulgate standards of professional conduct regarding the prescribing of drugs over the Internet. Several other professional associations, such as the American

Medical Association (AMA), have also established policies regarding the safe practice of online medicine. For example, the AMA guidelines, like the FSMB guidelines, state that doctors should perform a physical evaluation of patients before prescribing medication and should be licensed in every state in which their patients reside. The AMA guidelines further advise against prescribing drugs to patients solely on the basis of online communications such as questionnaires. American Medical Association, *Guidance for Physicians on Internet Prescribing (H-120.949)* (2003), at http://www.ama-assn.org/.

In: Health Care Crisis in America
Editor: Janet B. Prince, pp. 77-102

ISBN: 1-59454-689-4
© 2006 Nova Science Publishers, Inc.

Chapter 4

HEALTH INSURANCE: A PRIMER[*]

Bernadette Fernandez

SUMMARY

People buy insurance to protect themselves against possible financial loss in the future. Such losses may be due to a motor vehicle collision, natural disaster, or other circumstance. For patients, financial losses may result from the use of medical services. Health insurance then provides protection against the possibility of financial loss due to health care use. In addition, since people do not know ahead of time exactly what their health care expenses will be, paying for health insurance on a regular basis helps smooth out their spending.

While health insurance continues to be mainly a private enterprise in this country, government plays an increasingly significant role. Especially during the latter half of the 20th century, the government both initiated and responded to dynamics in medicine, the economy, and the workplace through legislation and public policies. For example, the Internal Revenue Service clarified that employer contributions to employee health benefits are exempt from taxation, which encouraged the growth of employment-based health coverage. Given the frequent introduction of legislation aimed at modifying or building on the current health insurance system, understanding the potential impact of such proposals requires a working knowledge of how

---

[*] Excerpted from CRS Report for Congress RL32237, Updated February 3, 2005.

health insurance is designed, provided, purchased, and regulated. This article provides basic information about those topics.

Persons and families without health coverage are more likely than those with coverage to forgo needed health care, which often leads to worse health outcomes and the need for expensive medical treatment. Since uninsured persons are more likely to be poor than insured persons, the uninsured are less able to afford the health care they need. Uninsurance can lead to health care access problems for communities, such as overcrowding in emergency rooms. Furthermore, individual states and the nation as a whole are affected through increased taxes and health care prices to cover uncompensated care expenses.

Americans obtain health insurance in different settings and through a variety of methods. People may get health coverage through the private sector, or from a publicly funded program. Consumers may purchase health insurance on their own, as part of an employee group, or through a trade or professional association. A small minority of employees get health insurance at no up-front cost because their employer pays the total insurance premium. However, 45 million Americans did not have health coverage for the entire year of 2003.

Health insurance benefits are delivered and financed under different systems. The factors that distinguish one delivery system from another are many, including how health care is financed, how much access to providers and services is controlled, and how much authority the enrollee has to design her/his health plan. To illustrate, managed care is characterized by predetermined restrictions on accessing services, whereas individual decision-making regarding use of health benefits is a hallmark of consumer-driven health care. And as economic conditions change, a specific delivery system may gain or lose the interest of affected parties.

INTRODUCTION

Health insurance coverage dominates many state and federal health care discussions. As health coverage evolved from an uncommon benefit to a routine one, government's role in subsidizing and regulating that coverage also changed for workers, employers, and insurers. Although health insurance continues to be mainly a private enterprise in this country, public entities play an increasingly significant role.

Government's involvement in health coverage expanded dramatically in the latter half of the 20th century. Public policies and legislation initiated or responded to dynamics in medicine, employment, and other areas.

- A long-standing rule issued by the Internal Revenue Service (IRS) stated that an employer's contributions to employment-based health insurance could not be included in an employee's gross income for tax purposes (Internal Revenue Code, Section 106). This ruling helped spur the growth of employer-sponsored health benefits. The IRS also stated separately that employers could deduct such contributions as part of business expenses.
- Advances in medicine led to escalating consumer demand for newer, better treatments. At the same time the cost of health care increased, which was especially problematic for certain groups of care consumers who lacked health coverage. This led to government efforts to assist consumers in paying for health care through social insurance programs.[1]
- More and more employees began to work for more than one employer over their lifetimes. Government was called on to address a problem many workers faced: keeping health coverage as they moved from job to job.

Given the frequent introduction of legislation aimed at modifying or building on the current health insurance system, understanding the potential impact of such proposals requires a working knowledge of how health insurance is designed, provided, purchased, and regulated. This article provides basic information about those topics.

WHAT IS HEALTH INSURANCE?

Basic Definitions and Principles

People buy insurance to protect themselves against possible financial loss in the future. Such losses may be due to a motor vehicle collision, natural disaster, or other circumstance. For patients, financial losses may result from the use of medical services. Health insurance then provides protection against the possibility of financial loss due to health care use. In addition, since people do not know ahead of time exactly what their health care expenses will be, paying for health insurance on a regular basis helps smooth out their spending.

The concept underlying insurance is "risk;" i.e., the likelihood and magnitude of financial loss. In any type of insurance arrangement, all parties seek to minimize their own risk. In health insurance, consumers and insurers approach the management of insurance risk differently. From the consumer's point of view, a person (or family) buys health insurance for protection against financial losses resulting from the future use of medical care. From the insurer's point of view, it employs a variety of methods to minimize the risk it takes on when providing health coverage to consumers, so as to assure that it operates a profitable business. One method is to cover only those expenses arising from a pre-defined set of services (generally called "covered" services). Another method for limiting risk is to encourage healthier people to obtain health coverage, presumably because healthier people would not need as many medical services as sicker people.

While the methods employed by an insurer differ from those of a consumer, each person or entity has the same goal: to minimize risk in an uncertain future. It is this uncertainty of the future and risk of loss which form the context for insurance, and the strategies to make financial loss more predictable and manageable which drive insurance arrangements.

Uneven Distribution of Health Care Expenses

In health care, a minority of consumers are responsible for a majority of expenses. According to a study that looked at the distribution of health care spending, 5% of the population accounted for over half of all health expenditures, and 10% of the population accounted for around two-thirds of those expenditures.[2] Such findings were consistent for selected years spanning three decades. Given the unevenness of health care spending and the impossibility of identifying all of the highest spenders before they use medical services, insurers employ various strategies in order to minimize the risk they take on.

Risk Pool and Rate Setting

The main objective of insurance is to spread risk across a group of people. This objective is achieved in health insurance when people contribute to a common pool ("risk pool") an amount at least equal to the average *expected* cost resulting from use of covered services by the group as a whole. In this way, the *actual* costs of health services used by a few people are spread over the entire group. This is the reason why insuring larger groups is considered less risky — the more persons participating in a risk pool, the less likely that the serious medical experiences of one or a few persons will result in catastrophic financial loss for the entire pool.

An insurer calculates and charges a rate (i.e., a "premium") in order to finance the health coverage it provides. The premium generally reflects several factors, including the expected cost of claims for using services in a year, administrative expenses associated with running the plan, and a risk or "profit" charge. The premium also will vary depending on if it buys self-only coverage or family coverage (see later discussion). If the insurer accurately estimates future costs and sets appropriate premium levels, then claims for that risk pool should be reasonably predictable over time. In other words, the premiums paid by healthy persons in the risk pool help subsidize the costs of less healthy persons.

Risk Pool Composition and Adverse Selection

As noted above, one of the ways insurers attempt to make future costs more predictable is by spreading the risk of high costs for a few people across many people. But the number of people is not the only significant factor. Equally as important, if not more so, is the composition of the group.

A consumer's decision to obtain health coverage is based on a variety of factors, such as health status, estimated need for future medical care, and disposable income. Consumers with different health conditions, as well as varying degrees of comfort towards risk-taking, will differ on whether they consider health insurance necessary. This is a circumstance that insurers will consider when estimating the cost to cover future health care use. With this in mind, insurers generally will vary the premiums they charge and the health services they cover (subject to state and federal statues) in order to attract various segments of the population. This flexibility in rate setting and benefit determination is particularly important in a competitive insurance market where insurers try to provide the most attractive rates to increase their market share.

However, some risk pools do attract a disproportionate share of unhealthy individuals. In part, this is because people generally know more about their own health conditions than any other person or entity, such as an insurer. Health care consumers typically are the best informed about when they will need medical care and what kind of services they will need. The "information asymmetry" between what consumers know compared to what insurers know gives consumers an advantage when looking for health coverage that will meet their future demand for health care. This asymmetry is another source of uncertainty which insurers take into account when developing and pricing insurance products (or health plans).

When a disproportionate share of unhealthy people make up a risk pool, a phenomenon known as "adverse selection," the average cost for each person in the pool rises. The higher costs may encourage the departure of healthier members from the group, and discourage the entrance of other healthy people, since healthier people may be able to find cheaper coverage elsewhere, or decide that coverage is too costly and become uninsured. In either situation, it leaves an even less healthy group of people in the risk pool, which again causes the average cost to rise for the remaining participants. If there is no change in this dynamic, the group may experience a "death spiral" as it suffers substantial adverse selection leading to an increasingly expensive risk pool and possibly dissolution of the pool altogether. Therefore, despite the consumer's information advantage, it does not guarantee access to affordable and adequate health coverage.

Group Market, Nongroup Market, and Medical Underwriting

Health insurance can be provided to groups of people that are drawn together by an employer or other organization, such as a professional association or trade union. Such groups are generally formed for some purpose other than obtaining insurance, like employment. When insurance is provided to a group, it is referred to as "group coverage" or "group insurance." In the group insurance market, the entity that purchases health insurance on behalf of a risk pool is referred to as the "sponsor."

Consumers who are not associated with a group can obtain health coverage by purchasing it directly from an insurer in the individual (or nongroup) insurance market. Insurance carriers in the nongroup market conduct an exhaustive analysis of *each* applicant's insurability. An applicant usually must provide the insurer with an extensive medical history and often undergo a physical exam. This information is used by carriers to assess the potential medical claims for each person by comparing characteristics of the applicant to the loss experience of others with similar characteristics. Once such an evaluation has been conducted, the carrier decides whether or not to provide health coverage and determines the conditions for coverage. This evaluation and determination process is called "underwriting."

Medical underwriting is standard practice in the individual insurance market, though a carrier's ability to reject applicants or vary the terms of coverage are restricted to some degree by federal and state requirements. In the group insurance market, insurers forgo underwriting in the traditional sense; i.e., reviewing *each* person's demographics and medical history. Instead, an insurer looks at the characteristics of the collective group — such as its claims history, demographics (e.g., industry of firm and age distribution of enrollees), and geographic location —to conduct the insurance risk and loss analysis. The insurer then charges a premium based on the analysis of the group's characteristics. There are exceptions to this for very small groups. For example, when a firm with only a handful of employees applies for health coverage, the insurer may choose to review the health conditions of each person in order to establish a premium for the entire group. Or, the insurer may charge a larger premium due to the larger risk attributed to smaller groups, if permitted under law.[3]

Fully Insured vs. Self-Insured Plans

A common distinction made between types of health insurance products is whether they are fully insured or self-insured. A fully insured health plan is one in which the sponsor purchases health coverage from a state-licensed insurer (also referred to as an insurance carrier). The carrier assumes the risk of providing covered services to the sponsor's enrolled members. In contrast, organizations who self-insure (or self-fund) do *not* purchase health coverage from state-licensed insurers. Self-insured plans refer to health coverage that is provided directly by the organization (e.g., employing firm) seeking coverage for its members (e.g., employees). Such organizations directly take on the risk for covering medical expenses, and such plans are not subject to state insurance regulations. Thus, a large employer that self-funds employee health benefits acts as both sponsor and insurer for that coverage. Firms that self-fund typically contract with third-party administrators (TPAs) to handle administrative duties such as member services, premium collection, and utilization review. TPAs do not underwrite insurance risk.

Self-only vs. Family Coverage

Another common distinction made in health insurance is whether the policy covers one person or a family. Under self-only coverage, the holder of the insurance policy is the only person insured. (Self-only coverage sometimes is referred to as individual coverage. Individual coverage in this sense should not be confused with health coverage from the individual insurance market — see discussion below.) Family coverage applies to the policyholder, her/his spouse, and children.[4] Self-only and family policies may differ from each other in terms of the services they cover and the cost-sharing they impose.

Administrative Expenses

Costs for administrative functions encompass a wide range of operational activities. Administrative expenses include costs associated with contracting with providers, sales and marketing, enrollment and billing, customer service, utilization review, case management, and other functions. The estimate of administrative expenses as a percent of claims often is used as a measure of operational efficiency. For large firms that self-insure, administrative costs make up 5-11% of claims, compared with 33-37% for insurers of small firms.[5] In the nongroup market, administrative expenses are often higher on a per-person basis compared to the group market.

TAX PREFERENCE

Unlike most industrialized countries, the United States does not guarantee health coverage to all of its citizens. Instead, it relies on a patchwork approach that combines private and public means for providing and accessing health insurance and health care. One of the key pieces of this approach encouraged the growth of employment-based health coverage via the tax code.

Section 106 of the Internal Revenue Code states that employer contributions to employment-based health insurance are not included in employees' gross incomes for tax purposes. This tax preference encourages workers to sign up for ("take-up") health coverage within the work setting. A separate ruling by the Internal Revenue Service clarified that such employer contributions are business expenses and, therefore, deductible from employers' taxable income. Both parties benefit: employers use health insurance coverage as a means to recruit and retain workers, while employees typically get access to more services at better rates (see discussion below). However, employees generally receive reduced wages to compensate for richer fringe benefits.

The tax exclusion of fringe benefits is one of the primary reason why health coverage is provided mainly through the workplace in this country. Approximately two out of three nonelderly (under 65) Americans have employment-sponsored insurance (ESI). Moreover, of nonelderly persons with private health insurance coverage, approximately nine out of 10 obtain it through the workplace.

HEALTH INSURANCE REGULATION

Regulation occurs at multiple points in the process of providing health coverage. Health insurance regulation addresses a wide variety of issues: the benefits that must be offered, the individuals to whom the insurance is made available, and the responsibilities insurers have to their health plan enrollees are a few of those issues. The most common distinction (and one of the most contentious areas) in the regulation of health insurance is whether it is the responsibility of individual states or the federal government. This distinction is important because federal and state laws governing health plans differ on issues such as compensation in courts, access to care, and mandated coverage for certain benefits.

Responsibility of the States

The regulation of insurance traditionally has been a state responsibility, as clarified by the 1945 McCarran-Ferguson Act. However, overlapping federal requirements complicate the matter with respect to health insurance. Individual states have established standards and regulations overseeing the "business of insurance," including requirements related to the finances, management, and business practices of an insurer. For example, all states have laws that require state-licensed insurance carriers to offer coverage for specified health care services (known as "mandated benefits"). Because fully insured plans are subject to state-established requirements, those plans must offer those mandated benefits. On the other hand, self-insured plans are not subject to state insurance regulations so they are exempt from such requirements.

Key Federal Statutes

Regardless of whether health plans are fully insured or self-funded, they all are subject to a number of federal laws (e.g., the Americans with Disabilities Act). Two of these federal laws, the Employee Retirement Income Security Act of 1974 (ERISA, P.L. 93-406) and the Health Insurance Portability and Accountability Act of 1996 (HIPAA, P.L. 104-191), have significant impact on how health insurance is provided.

ERISA outlines minimum federal standards for private-sector employer-sponsored benefits. (Public employee benefits and plans sponsored by churches generally are exempt from ERISA). Passed in response to pension abuses, the Act was developed with a focus on pensions, but the law applies to a long list of "welfare benefits" including health insurance. The Act requires that funds be handled prudently and in the best interest of beneficiaries, participants be informed of their rights, and there be adequate disclosure of a plan's financial activities. ERISA preempts state laws for issues that "relate to" employee benefit plans. (In other words, the federal law overrides state laws affecting private-sector employee benefits). This portion of ERISA was designed to ensure that plans would be subject to the same benefit laws across all states, partly in consideration of firms that operate in multiple states. However, state laws still apply for issues which involve the "business of insurance." Given the ambiguity of the phrases "relate to" and "business of insurance," the ERISA preemption is an area of heated debate and active litigation.[6]

The core motivation behind the Health Insurance Portability and Accountability Act of 1996 (HIPAA) is to address the concern that insured persons have about losing their coverage if they switch jobs or change health plans ("portability" of health coverage). The Act's health insurance provisions established federal requirements on private and public employer-sponsored health plans and insurers. It ensures the availability and renewability of coverage for certain employees and other persons under specified circumstances. HIPAA limits the amount of time that coverage for pre-existing medical conditions can be denied, and prohibits discrimination on the basis of health status-related factors. The Act also includes tax provisions designed to encourage the expansion of health coverage through several mechanisms, such as a demonstration project for tax-advantaged medical savings accounts and a graduated increase of the portion of premiums self-employed persons could deduct from their federal income tax calculations. Another set of HIPAA provisions addresses the electronic transmission of health information and the privacy of personally identifiable medical information (administrative simplification and privacy provisions, respectively).[7]

WHY IS HEALTH INSURANCE CONSIDERED IMPORTANT?

While health insurance coverage is not necessary to obtain health care, it is a vital mechanism for accessing services in an environment of increasingly expensive health care. As health care costs rise — at times outstripping the rise in wages —more people need greater assistance with covering medical expenses. Health insurance provides some measure of protection for consumers, especially those who have limited means or greater-than-average need for medical care.

Health insurance is considered important also because of the well-documented, far-reaching consequences of uninsurance. For instance, uninsured persons are more likely to forgo needed health care than people with health coverage. This includes forgoing services for preventable or chronic conditions which often leads to worse health outcomes.[8] Uninsured persons also are less likely to have a "usual source of care;" i.e., a person or place identified as the source to which the patient *usually* goes for health services or medical advice (not including emergency rooms). In 2002, while only one-tenth of all adults with private health insurance identified no usual source of care, almost half of all uninsured adults had no usual source.[9] Having a usual source is important because people who establish ongoing relationships with health care providers or facilities are more likely than persons without a usual source to access preventive health services and have regular visits with a physician.[10] Therefore, to the extent that health insurance coverage facilitates access to medical services, people without coverage face substantial barriers in the pursuit of the health care they need.

The negative consequences of uninsurance extends beyond the persons directly involved. The Institute of Medicine found that the insurance status of parents affects the amount of health care their children receive.[11] In places with crowded emergency rooms, increasing uninsurance rates can add to that problem, since uninsured persons have fewer places from which they can get general health services outside of emergency departments (EDs), compared to people with health coverage. Overcrowding in EDs, in turn, leads to longer waits for all patients seeking emergency care. Moreover, many uninsured persons forgo preventive health care and end up developing more serious conditions requiring complex, expensive medical services. Since health coverage is positively related to income, uninsured persons are less likely to be able to afford this level of care. In cases where patients are unable to cover the costs associated with receiving health services, the facilities that provided those services must take it as a financial loss (i.e., uncompensated care). These losses can be staggering. For example, one study estimated that health care providers gave approximately $35 billion of uncompensated care to the uninsured in 2001.[12]

Ultimately, though, the costs for caring for the uninsured are "passed down to all taxpayers and consumers of health care in the form of higher taxes and higher prices for services and insurance."[13] Taxpayers are affected because the federal government makes payments to hospitals — for patients enrolled in certain programs — which take into account the share of poor people treated. The assumption is that facilities that treat a larger proportion of poor people have a greater problem with uninsurance and uncompensated care. The federal government also provides grants to many health centers and other facilities that serve poor communities. In addition, states and localities fund local health programs, public hospitals, and clinics —facilities that generally serve an uninsured (or medically underserved) population. Health care consumers are affected by uninsurance because in order for physician practices and hospitals to survive financially they have to make-up the losses they sustain. Hospitals and physicians may raise rates for certain services or discontinue unprofitable programs in order to recoup those losses, thereby affecting consumers' pocketbooks and access to services. Uninsurance, then, has negative health and financial consequences for uninsured persons, their families, communities, states, and the nation as a whole.

WHERE DO PEOPLE GET HEALTH INSURANCE?

Americans obtain health insurance in different settings and through a variety of methods (see **Table 1**). People may get it through the private sector, or from a publicly funded social insurance program. Consumers may purchase health coverage on their own, as part of an employee group, or through a trade or professional association. A small minority of employees get health insurance at no up-front cost because their employer pays the total insurance premium (both the employee and employer shares of the premium). However, 45 million Americans did not have health coverage for the entire year of 2003.[14]

Employer-Sponsored Insurance

Even though examples of health insurance in this country stretch back almost 200 years, most Americans did not have health coverage until the latter half of the 20th century.[15] The demand for more workers during World War II and a wage freeze imposed by the National War Labor Board generated great interest in employer-sponsored insurance (ESI) as a worker recruitment and retention tool.[16] Buoyed by legislation and court rulings declaring the tax exemption of fringe benefits, and support from unions for work-based coverage, health insurance became a pervasive employment benefit.

In employer-sponsored insurance, risk pools may be comprised of active workers, dependents, and retirees. Insurers use a number of strategies to increase the likelihood that each risk pool includes a good proportion of healthy individuals, thus avoiding adverse selection. For instance, insurers may restrict employees' opportunities to take-up health coverage or switch health plans by designating a specific time frame each year for such activities ("open enrollment period"). Such a strategy decreases the likelihood that people will "game" the system by taking up coverage only when they plan on using health services (e.g., for pregnancy and birth), and dropping coverage when they no longer plan to access care. Insurers also may require the employer to enroll a certain proportion of the firm's eligible population. Assuming that the eligible population consists of a good percentage of healthy people, requiring a certain proportion of all eligibles to enroll leads to an enrollee population which contains at least some healthy people.

Table 1. Health Insurance Coverage by Type of Insurance, 2003

	Coverage distribution	Millions of persons
Total population	100.0%	288.3
Employment Based	61.8	178.2
Nongroup	9.2	26.5
Medicare	13.7	39.5
Medicaid/SCHIP/State programs	12.4	35.7
Military/Veterans Coverage	3.5	10.1
No health insurance	15.6	45.0

Source: CRS Report 96-891 EPW, Health Insurance Coverage: Characteristics of the Insured and Uninsured Populations in 2003, by Chris Peterson.

Note: The most-current data on health insurance coverage for a full year is for the year 2003. Columns do not add to totals because persons may receive insurance coverage from more than one source.

Employers also use strategies to encourage insurance take-up by healthy people. For example, employers usually pay part (or, in very few instances, all) of the total premium. This practice makes health coverage a more attractive benefit, even to those who do not plan to use medical services on a regular basis. Overall, insurers may assume that not all people in ESI risk pools take-up health coverage for reasons primarily related to personal health status or immediate demand for medical care.

Advantages

ESI plans retain enrollees better than the individual health insurance market. As previously mentioned, health benefits provided at the workplace are exempt from income and employment taxes, encouraging the growth and continuity of employer-sponsored health insurance. Large risk pools with a good proportion of healthy enrollees tend to be more stable than small pools or those with a higher proportion of unhealthy enrollees. Given the strategies discussed above to discourage adverse selection, insurers assume that ESI pools — particularly large, diverse ones — are more stable. Generally, this translates into less volatile costs and better overall rates in the group market compared to the nongroup market. Also, large ESI groups can use their size to negotiate for better benefits and cost-sharing, in contrast to individual applicants in the nongroup market. Plan sponsors negotiate and interact with insurers on behalf of all of their insured members, unlike in the individual market where each consumer must deal with the insurance carrier directly in order to apply for and purchase coverage. In addition, there are economies of scale for enrollees in the group market compared to the nongroup market for such administrative activities such as sales, billing, and customer service. For these reasons, workers and their families benefit from receiving coverage through the workplace. For plan sponsors, the main advantage is to use health coverage to recruit and retain workers. This is particularly appealing in a growing economy — such as during most of the 1990s — when there may be high demand for workers.

Disadvantages

While there are many advantages to obtaining ESI coverage, there are challenges as well. From the vantage point of the enrollee, one of the biggest disadvantages is the general lack of portability. Because ESI coverage is tied to the job and not the person, any change in employment (such as going from full-time to part-time status, or changing jobs) may alter the health care providers or services to which the worker has access, or disrupt health coverage altogether. Also, in firms that offer health coverage, there is a trade off made between wages and benefits. For workers who do not take up health insurance from those firms, they end up accepting lower wages for a set of benefits they do not access. From the perspective of the sponsor, an underlying challenge is the lack of enrollee awareness of the true costs of health care. Because the sponsor contributes to the cost of the premium, enrollees do not bear the full cost of obtaining health coverage. More importantly, enrollees generally do not have to cover the entire cost of the services they use, since sponsors negotiate for lower rates and better cost-sharing arrangements from insurers. Consumers enrolled in managed care plans in particular are shielded from health care's true costs. Some observers contend that this lack of cost awareness gives little incentive to consumers to utilize medical services prudently, which leads to greater use of services and greater overall health care expenditures. In addition, sponsors' efforts to constrain their health care spending — by increasing the employee share of the premium or employee cost-sharing — are made even more difficult to justify or implement. Finally, from the perspective of the federal budget, the tax exclusion of employer-sponsored health insurance represents a lost source for Treasury funds.

Large vs. Small Groups

The group insurance market often is thought of as consisting of large and small groups. The underlying reason for this distinction is rooted in the inverse relationship between insurance risk and group size; i.e., the risk associated with a group grows as the size of the group shrinks. This concept affects employers' offers of health benefits. For instance, a very large employer often is able to offer multiple health plan options to its members (e.g., the Federal Employee Health Benefit Program (FEHBP)). A large business can leverage its size to get a more comprehensive set of benefits. On the other hand, small employers are less able to provide health coverage at all because of the greater risk associated with small groups. Even when small employers do offer coverage, the benefits are often limited. Small employers also are much less likely to self-fund health coverage, since there is a smaller pool for spreading risk and protecting against catastrophic loss. Furthermore, such entities generally do not have the necessary administrative capacity to negotiate with multiple provider groups and handle all the day-to-day operational functions conducted by insurers. It is conditions such as these which prompt legislators to develop proposals for expanding small group participation in health insurance; for example, targeting association health plans and health marts, and opening up FEHBP to the small group market.

Association health plans and health marts are examples of the spectrum of entities which bring groups of people together for the purpose of buying health insurance. These entities include trade and professional associations that offer health coverage to their members ("association-sponsored plans"), and small firms that band together to purchase coverage as a group ("health insurance purchasing cooperatives"). The premise behind pooling arrangements is to decrease the administrative burden on and increase the negotiating capacity of participants who cannot afford to offer or purchase coverage on their own. Around one-third of small firms buy health coverage through some type of purchasing pool.[17]

Public Programs

While most Americans with health insurance obtain it through the private-sector, tens of millions of people get their medical care paid for through public programs. Below are descriptions of selected federal and state programs which provide payments on behalf of many persons who, due to low incomes or high health care expenses, could not afford health care otherwise.

Medicare

The Medicare program was established in 1965, and is a federal program for seniors (65 years and older), certain nonelderly persons with disabilities, and persons with end-stage renal (kidney) disease. Medicare currently consists of three parts: Part A, Hospital Insurance; Part B, Supplementary Medical Insurance; and Part C, Medicare Advantage, formerly referred to as the Medicare+Choice program. Together, Parts A and B cover many medical services, such as care provided in hospitals and skilled nursing facilities, hospice care, home health care, physician services, physical and occupational therapy, and other services. The then Medicare+Choice program, added three decades after Medicare was established, was created to expand the availability and diversity of managed care plans that cover all Part A and B services. P.L. 108-173 added a new Part D to the Medicare program. Effective in 2006, Medicare beneficiaries may access outpatient prescription drug benefits through Part D.

A large majority of Americans age 65 and older are automatically entitled to coverage under Part A and do not have to pay a premium because either they or their spouse paid Medicare payroll taxes on their past earnings. (Even if an elderly person did not pay Medicare taxes, she/he may be able to purchase Part A coverage.) Part A also provides coverage for certain nonelderly persons who receive Social Security cash benefits. Enrollment in Medicare Part B is voluntary for eligible individuals. For most persons who are entitled to benefits under Part A, they are enrolled automatically in Part B, but they are given the option to decline coverage. The small minority of people who do not have automatic enrollment may request enrollment in writing. All Part B enrollees pay a monthly premium for coverage.

Since its creation in the mid-1960s, Medicare has provided health coverage to tens of millions of Americans, and in 2003 had 40 million enrollees. The program has been so successful in covering the elderly that the problem of uninsurance usually is described in terms of the under-65 population.

Medicaid and the State Children's Health Insurance Program (SCHIP)

Medicaid is the main health insurance program for very low-income Americans. It provides coverage for health care and long-term-care services to certain adults (generally parents and pregnant women), children, the elderly, and persons with disabilities. Medicaid is jointly funded by federal and state governments, and is administered by the states within federally set guidelines. State Medicaid programs provide a comprehensive set of services, reflecting its diverse enrollee population. These programs must provide a set of federally specified benefits, such as hospital services (both inpatient and outpatient), physician services, nursing home care, home health care for those entitled to services from nursing facilities, and certain services for children. States also have the authority to cover additional services. Some states have used their waiver authority under Medicaid to extend coverage to uninsured persons who could not meet the program's financial tests. Medicaid is a means-tested program and applicants must meet financial and other criteria in order to be eligible for program services. Everyone who meets the eligibility criteria is entitled to Medicaid benefits.

The State Children's Health Insurance Program was established in 1997 to allow states to cover certain low-income children. In designing their programs, states can choose among three options: expand Medicaid, create a new "separate state" insurance program, or devise a combination of both approaches. States that choose to expand Medicaid to SCHIP eligibles must provide the full range of Medicaid benefits, as well as all optional services specified in their state Medicaid plans. States that establish SCHIP programs that are separate from Medicaid choose one of three benefit options. All 50 states, the District of Columbia, and five territories have established some type of SCHIP program. SCHIP's eligibility rules target uninsured children under 19 years of age whose families' incomes are above Medicaid eligibility levels. States may raise the upper income level for low-income children up to 200% of the federal poverty level, or higher under certain circumstances.[18]

Individual Health Insurance

The individual insurance ("nongroup") market is often referred to as a "residual" market. The reason being that this market provides coverage to persons who cannot obtain health insurance through the workplace and do not qualify for public programs such as Medicare, Medicaid, or SCHIP.

Consequently, the enrollee population for this private health insurance market is small.

The residual nature of the nongroup market is evident in the demographic makeup of those who purchase coverage from it. The market is over-represented by the near elderly (55-64 years old); a group that has relatively weak attachments to the workplace. The individual market disproportionately consists of part-time workers, part-year workers, and the self-employed, groups unlikely to have access to ESI coverage.[19] Also, some people use the nongroup market as a temporary source of coverage, such as those in-between jobs or early retirees who are not yet eligible for Medicare.

Applicants to the individual insurance market must go through robust underwriting. Insurance carriers in most states conduct an exhaustive analysis of each applicant's insurability. An applicant usually must provide her/his medical history, and often undergo a physical exam. This information is used by carriers to assess the potential medical claims for each person. Federal and state requirements restrict somewhat insurers' ability to reject applications or design coverage based on health factors (such as benefit exclusions for certain pre-existing health conditions). Nonetheless, some applicants are rejected from the nongroup market altogether, and others who are approved may receive limited benefits or are charged premiums that are higher than those in the group market for similar coverage.[20] Rigorous underwriting results in an enrollee population that is fairly healthy (three out of four enrollees report that their health is excellent or very good),[21] thereby excluding persons with moderate to severe health problems from the private nongroup insurance market.

State High-Risk Pools

Many states have high-risk pools, which are nonprofit entities that provide health coverage to persons with high health care expenses. Generally, such persons are denied coverage in the individual insurance market because of their health conditions and/or predicted use of costly medical services. If they are not eligible for public programs (e.g., their incomes may exceed the financial eligibility criteria), they have very few options for obtaining care. As of December 2003, 32 states run high-risk health insurance pools.[22] These programs tend to be small and eligibility varies by state. While some state high-risk pools have successfully provided health coverage to high-risk people, many programs are beset by accessibility, adequacy, and affordability problems.[23]

The Uninsured

Despite the various private and public sources of health insurance, millions of Americans are without health coverage. In 2003, 45 million people were without health insurance coverage for the entire year.[24] For the vast majority of the uninsured, they lack coverage because they cannot *access* coverage (e.g., their employer does not offer health insurance as an employment benefit) or they cannot *afford* it.

Uninsurance is characterized as a problem of the under-65 population, given the near-universal coverage of seniors through Medicare. The nonelderly uninsured population differs from the insured population on a number of key demographic factors. One of the most striking characteristic of persons who lack coverage is that a significant proportion are in low-income families. For instance, among all uninsured persons under age 65, two-thirds were in poor or near poor families in 2003.[25] Moreover, among nonelderly persons who are poor, a full one-third lacked health insurance coverage, compared to less than one-fifth of the poor who received coverage through the workplace.[26]

A defining characteristic of the nonelderly uninsured population is that over 80% are persons with ties to the paid labor force, or dependents of such persons. Even more surprising is that over half of the nonelderly uninsured were workers with full-time, full-year status, or the dependents of those workers. While such findings may be counter-intuitive, there are multiple reasons why employed persons and their families may lack health coverage. For example, a worker may be offered health insurance by his/her employer, but declines it because he/she thinks it is too expensive. An employee may work for a small firm which is less likely than a large firm to offer health insurance as a benefit. A low-wage employee, even working full time, is less likely to be offered health insurance at work and less likely to be able to afford it than higher-wage workers in the same firm. Finally, a healthy worker may be willing to take on the risk of being uninsured and choose not to purchase insurance. Despite the dominance of employer-sponsored health insurance, the dynamics of work, insurance risk, and financial resources intersect to impede the coverage of all workers and their families.

The problem of the uninsured is a paramount health care concern to many policymakers and legislators. One of the topics of ongoing debate is the overall number of uninsured and the direction of the uninsurance rate. These issues have generated some controversy over dueling analyses which show slightly different (and sometimes, moderately different) findings. But despite the forceful discussions regarding trends in uninsurance, the year-to-year changes in the uninsurance rate actually are small. For example, from 1987 to 2003 (the last year of available data), the change in the annual uninsurance rate usually was one-half of 1% or less.[27] Nonetheless, tens of millions of Americans were without coverage during that time period. Such circumstances beg the questions: why does pervasive uninsurance persist (even during the robust economy of the mid-1990s), and what are the implications for legislation and public policies to expand health coverage?

HOW ARE HEALTH BENEFITS DELIVERED AND FINANCED?

Given the complexity of the health care system overall, it is no surprise that health benefits are delivered and financed through different arrangements. Those arrangements vary due to numerous factors such as: how health care is financed, how much access to providers and services are controlled, and how much authority the enrollee has to design her/his health plan. While delivery systems may share certain characteristics, general distinctions can be made based on payment, access, and other critical variables.

Indemnity (Traditional) Insurance

Under indemnity insurance, the insured person decides when and from whom to seek health services. If the services the enrollee receives are covered under his/her insurance, the enrollee or the enrollee's provider files a claim with the insurer. Thus, insurers make payments *retrospectively* (i.e., after the health services have been rendered), up to the maximum amounts specified for each covered service. In this model of health care delivery, the financing of health services and the obtaining of those services are kept separate.

This bifurcated arrangement was unquestioned for a time. But as medical costs began to rise, sometimes faster than other sectors of the national economy, many observers criticized this delivery model as contributing to increasing expenses. Because providers were compensated on a fee-for-service basis, some argued that providers were not given incentives to provide efficient health care. In fact, some critics accused health care practitioners and institutions of providing an overabundance of health care in order to generate greater revenue. By the early 1970s, legislators, analysts, and others expressed considerable interest in alternative models, such as managed care models, with cost control as a key feature.

Managed Care

While managed care means different things to different people, several key characteristics set it apart from traditional (indemnity) insurance. One of the main differences is that the service delivery and financing functions are integrated under managed care. Managed care organizations (MCOs) employ various techniques to control costs and manage health service use *prospectively*. Among those techniques are restricting enrollee access to certain providers ("in-network" providers); requiring primary-care-physician approval for access to specialty care ("gatekeeping"); coordinating care for persons with certain conditions ("disease management" or "case management"); and requiring prior authorization for routine hospital inpatient care ("pre-certification"). MCOs may offer different types of health plans that vary in the degree to which cost and medical decision-making is controlled. As a consequence, enrollee cost-sharing also varies. Generally, the more tightly managed a plan is, the less the premium charged. Other distinguishing features of the managed care approach include an emphasis on preventive health care and implementation of quality assurance processes.

Managed care was touted as the antidote to rapidly rising health care costs. Starting with the passage of federal legislation in the 1970s which supported the growth of managed care (specifically in the form of health maintenance organizations (HMOs)), the number of MCOs grew quickly. Increased market competition among these organizations led to decreases in premiums, in order to gain market share. With high medical inflation in the 1980s and early 1990s, enrollees flocked to these less-costly managed care plans. By the mid-1990s, more insured workers were enrolled in HMOs than any other health plan type, and health insurance premiums had stabilized.

But in the latter half of the 1990s, a "backlash" of sorts against managed care grew.[28] Some enrollees had grown weary of provider and service restrictions. Many MCOs that had increased market share through artificially low premiums began to raise them in order to increase revenue.[29] Consumers and others accused the managed care industry of caring more about controlling costs than providing health care. Some providers resented the role managed care played in medical decision-making. Many enrollees began to leave HMOs. The industry responded by developing insurance products that were less-tightly managed, but more costly.

Some traditional HMOs widened their provider networks and eliminated the gatekeeping function, while employers began to offer plan types that were less tightly managed, such as preferred provider organizations (PPOs). In fact, by the end of the 1990s, more people with work-based health coverage were enrolled in PPOs than in HMOs.[30]

As the influence of managed care waned and health care costs began to rise at an increasing pace during the late 1990s, the impact on consumers began to be felt. For example, in the employment setting, employers absorbed the extra costs at first in order to recruit and retain workers during the booming economy of the mid to late 1990s.[31] But as the economy soured, employers began to pass these expenses along to enrollees in the form of greater cost-sharing.[32]

Consumer-Driven Health Plans

By the turn of the millennium, large increases in health costs again became commonplace. With the belief by some observers that the age of managed care was over, they began to search for alternatives. Consumer-driven (or consumer-directed) health plans have been offered as one such option.

Consumer-driven health care refers to a broad spectrum of approaches that give incentives to consumers to control their use of health services and/or ration their own health benefits. In the workplace, at one extreme employers may choose to provide an array of insurance products from which workers can choose, while at the other end an employer could increase wages but not offer any health coverage allowing workers to decide how to spend that extra money to meet their health care needs. Within those two endpoints, the consumer-directed approach varies in the degree to which consumers are responsible for health care decision-making.[33]

For example, one health benefits option that is at the heart of discussions about consumer-driven health care is the health savings account (HSA). Under this approach, the consumer is responsible for management of the account. HSAs are investment accounts in which contributions earn interest tax free. Consumers, their employers, or both may make contributions to HSAs. Consumers withdraw funds on a tax-free basis to cover medical expenses not covered by health insurance. Unused contributions roll over to the next year. HSAs must be paired with high-deductible health plans. If the HSA funds are exhausted and the deductible level has not been reached, the consumer is responsible for covering that gap. Once the consumer's spending reaches the deductible level, then coverage from the high-deductible plan takes effect.

While consumer-driven health care can take on many forms, the premise common to all of the approaches is that by making enrollees more responsible for their own health care, it creates incentives for people to use services prudently. The expectation is that greater cost-consciousness on the part of consumers will result in lower overall health costs. In essence, the service and cost control functions administered by MCOs and providers under managed care shifts to enrollees under the consumer-driven plan scenario.

Proponents of consumer-directed plans assert the merit in having people take increased responsibility for their own health care use and expenses. They predict that this approach will lead to better-informed consumers, more appropriate use of health services, and lower overall spending on health care. Opponents express concern that this approach does not recognize the possible range of health conditions in an enrolled population. They argue that these plans benefit the young and healthy who use relatively few services, and, therefore, would not need to expend a great deal of time and energy making these health care decisions. However, these plans impose a greater burden on individuals with moderate to severe health conditions because of their greater-than-average use of medical services.

REFERENCES

[1] Publicly funded health programs generally either provide funding for direct medical services or assist consumers in paying for health care. The latter are included in a broad category of programs based on "social insurance" principles. Social insurance refers to publicly funded insurance programs that are statutorily mandated for certain groups of people, such as low-income individuals.

[2] Marc L. Berk and Alan C. Monheit, "The Concentration of Health Care Expenditures, Revisited," *Health Affairs*, vol. 20, no. 2 (Mar./Apr. 2001), pp. 9-18.

[3] G. Claxton, "How Private Insurance Works: A Primer," Kaiser Family Foundation (KFF) website, Apr. 2002, at

[http://www.kff.org/Insurance/loader.cfm?url=/commonspot/security/getfile.cfm&PageID=14053]

[4] Policies vary on the requirements children must meet (e.g., age, martial status, etc.) in order to become eligible for or stay on a family policy.

[5] Rose C. Chu and Gordon R. Trapnell, "Study of the Administrative Costs and Actuarial Values of Small Health Plans," Small Business Research Summary no. 224, at [http://www.sba.gov/advo/research/rs224.pdf], Jan. 2003

[6] For more information about ERISA, see CRS Report RS20315, *ERISA Regulation of Health Plans: Fact Sheet*, by Hinda Chaikind.

[7] For more information about HIPAA, see CRS Report RL31634, *The Health Insurance Portability and Accountability Act (HIPAA) of 1996: Overview and Guidance on Frequently Asked Questions*, by Hinda Chaikind, Jean Hearne, Bob Lyke, Stephen Redhead and Julie Stone.

[8] Kaiser Commission on Medicaid and the Uninsured, "The Uninsured and Their Access to Health Care," KFF website at [http://www.kff.org/uninsured/loader.cfm?url=/commonspot/security/getfile.cfm&PageID=29284], Dec. 2003.

[9] National Center for Health Statistics, *Health, United States, 2004*.

[10] J. E. DeVoe et al., "Receipt of Preventive Care Among Adults: Insurance Status and Usual Source of Care," *American Journal of Public Health*, May 2003.

[11] Institute of Medicine, Committee on the Consequences of Uninsurance, *Coverage Matters: Insurance and Health Care*, 2001.

[12] J. Hadley and J. Holahan, "How Much Medical Care Do the Uninsured Use, and Who Pays for It?," Health Affairs Web Exclusive, Feb.12, 2003. The cost of uncompensated care for 2001 is the most-recent estimate on a national level.

[13] Institute of Medicine, Committee on the Consequences of Uninsurance, *A Shared Destiny*, 2003, p 122.

[14] .U.S. Census Bureau, *Current Population Survey*, 2004.

[15] See timeline from Employee Benefit Research Institute's (EBRI) "History of Health Insurance Benefits," EBRI website, Mar. 2002, at [http://www.ebri.org/facts/0302fact.htm].

[16] .Health Insurance Association of America, *Fundamentals of Health Insurance*, 1997.

[17] For additional information, see CRS Report RL31963, *Association Health Plans, Health Marts, and the Small Group Market for Health Insurance*, by Jean Hearne.

[18] For additional information about SCHIP, see CRS Report RL30473, *State Children's Health Insurance Program (SCHIP): A Brief Overview*, by Elicia J. Herz and Peter Kraut.
[19] D. J. Chollet, "Consumers, Insurers, and Market Behavior," *Journal of Health Politics, Policy and Law*, Feb. 2000.
[20] M. V. Pauly and A.M. Percy, "Cost and Performance: A Comparison of the Individual and Group Health Insurance Markets," *Journal of Health Politics, Policy and Law*, Feb. 2000.
[21] General Accounting Office, *Private Health Insurance: Millions Relying on Individual Market Face Cost and Coverage Trade-Offs*, Nov. 1996.
[22] States with high-risk pools: AL, AK, AR, CA, CO, CT, FL, ID, IL, IN, IA, KS, KY, LA, MD, MN, MS, MO, MT, NE, NH, NM, ND, OK, OR, SC, SD, TX, UT, WA, WI, and WY. A map of state high-risk pools is available at [http://www.statehealthfacts.org].
[23] For additional information about state high-risk pools, see CRS Report RL31745, *Health Insurance: State High-Risk Pools*, by Julie Stone.
[24] U.S. Census Bureau, *Current Population Survey*, 2004.
[25] According to the Census Bureau, the poverty level for a family of four was an annual income of $18,810 in 2003.
[26] For additional information, see CRS Report 96-891, *Health Insurance Coverage: Characteristics of the Insured and Uninsured Populations in 2003*, by Chris Peterson.
[27] .Data available at [http://www.census.gov/hhes/hlthins/historic/index.html].
[28] Richard Kronick, "Waiting for Godot: Wishes and Worries in Managed Care, " *Journal of Health Politics, Policy and Law*, vol. 24, no. 5 (Oct. 1999), pp. 1099-1106.
[29] Jon Gabel, et al., "Job-Based Health Insurance in 2001: Inflation Hits Double Digits, Managed Care Retreats," *Health Affairs*, vol. 20, no. 5 (Sept./Oct. 2001), pp. 180-186.
[30] American Association of Health Plans, "Health Plans and Employer-Sponsored Plans," Oct. 1999. Available at [http://www.ahip.org/content /default.aspx?bc=41|331|366].
[31] Jon B. Christianson and Sally Trude, "Managing Costs, Managing Benefits: Employer Decisions in Local Health Care Markets," *Health Services Research*, pt. II, vol. 38, no. 1, (Feb. 2003), pp. 357-373.
[32] Jon Gabel et al., "Job-Based Health Benefits in 2002: Some Important Trends," *Health Affairs*, vol. 21, no. 5 (Sept./Oct. 2002), pp. 143-151.

[33] P. Fronstin, ed., Employee Benefit Research Institute, *Consumer-Driven Health Benefits: A Continuing Evolution?* (Washington: EBRI, 2002).

In: Health Care Crisis in America
Editor: Janet B. Prince, pp. 103-110
ISBN: 1-59454-689-4
© 2006 Nova Science Publishers, Inc.

Chapter 5

HEALTH INSURANCE COVERAGE: CHARACTERISTICS OF THE INSURED AND UNINSURED POPULATIONS IN 2001[*]

Chris L. Peterson

SUMMARY

The number of Americans without health insurance rose in 2001 to 41.2 million Americans (14.6%) — an increase of 1.4 million people from 2000. This reversed a two-year trend of falling numbers of uninsured. Approximately 1.3 million fewer Americans had employment-based health coverage, compared to 2000, according to the Census Bureau. From 1999 to 2000, this number had risen by 2.9 million. In spite of the decline, most Americans (64.1%) still received their health insurance through an employer. Yet full-time, full-year workers and their family members made up more than half of the uninsured. The percentage of individuals covered by Medicaid increased significantly in 2001. Among children in 2001, the percentage of uninsured did not change significantly. This article examines characteristics of both the insured and the uninsured populations in the United States.

---

[*] Excerpted from CRS Report for Congress 96-891 EPW, Updated January 7, 2003.

HEALTH INSURANCE COVERAGE AND SELECTED POPULATION CHARACTERISTICS

Age

Table 1 provides a breakdown of health insurance coverage by type of insurance and age. In 2001, compared to other age groups, those under age 5 were most likely (29%) to have coverage through Medicaid, the State Children's Health Insurance Program (SCHIP), or some other program for low-income individuals. Young adults ages 19 to 24 were the most likely to have gone without health insurance for the entire year. While most in this age group (57%) were covered under an employment-based plan, 30% had no health insurance. Young adults are often too old to be covered as dependents on their parents' policies and, as entry-level workers, do not have strong ties to the work force. In addition, some may choose to remain uninsured and spend their money on other items. After age 25, the percentage of people without health insurance decreases. Of those age 65 and over, 96% were covered by Medicare, and less than 1% were uninsured for the entire year. The remainder of this article focuses on the population under age 65.

Table 1. Health Insurance Coverage by Type of Insurance and Ag

Age	Population (in millions)	Employment based[b]	Private nongroup	Medicare	Medicaid or other public[c]	Military/ veterans coverage	Uninsured
Under 5	19.4	60.8%	4.8%	0.7%	28.5%	3.5%	10.6%
5-18	57.1	66.3	5.1	0.6	20.2	3.2	12.6
19-24	23.4	57.3	6.0	0.7	9.6	2.7	29.7
25-34	38.7	66.2	5.3	1.3	6.7	2.1	23.4
35-54	83.8	74.4	6.8	2.6	5.5	2.7	14.7
55-61	19.3	70.4	9.9	7.1	7.0	4.3	12.8
62-64	6.5	61.9	12.9	14.2	6.9	5.9	14.1
65+	33.8	35.3	30.3	96.1	9.7	6.4	0.8
Total	**282.1**	**64.1%**	**9.2%**	**13.5%**	**11.2%**	**3.4%**	**14.6%**

Type of insurance[a]

Source: CRS analysis of data from the March 2002 Current Population Survey (CPS).
[a] People may have had more than one source of health insurance over the course of the year. [b] Group health insurance through employer or union. [c] Nonmilitary. Includes State Children's Health Insurance Program (SCHIP) and other state programs for low-income individuals.

Other Demographic Characteristics

Table 2 shows the rate of health insurance coverage by type of insurance and selected demographic characteristics — race, family type, region, poverty level and citizenship — *for people under age 65*. In 2001, whites were least likely to be uninsured (12%), while Hispanics were most likely (35%). The rate of employment-based health coverage was highest among whites (76%), and the rate of public coverage [1] was highest among blacks (24%).

People in male-headed or two-parent families with children were less likely to be uninsured (13%) than those in female-headed families with children (21%) or in families with no children (19%). The sources of coverage were quite different for male-present (one or two parents) and female-headed (single parent) families with children: coverage was employment based for 74% of male-present families compared to 45% of female-headed families; 10% of male-present families had public coverage compared to 36% of female-headed families.

People were less likely to be uninsured if they lived in the Midwest (12%) or the Northeast (14%), than if they lived in the South (19%) or West (19%). More than 70% of those living in the Northeast and Midwest had employment-based health insurance compared to 65% in the South and 63% in the West. Among individuals with incomes at least two times the poverty level, 11% went without health insurance compared to 34% of the poor (i.e., those with incomes below the poverty level). Only 21% of the poor received health coverage through employment, and 44% had public coverage. More than 80% of people with incomes at least two times the poverty level were covered through an employer, and only 5% had public coverage.

Non-citizens were more likely to be uninsured than people born with U.S. citizenship (i.e., "native") — 44% versus 14%, respectively. Non-citizens accounted for 8% of the population under 65, but were 21% of the uninsured. About 44% of non-citizens were covered through employment, compared to 70% of citizens.

Table 2. Health Insurance Coverage by Type of Insurance and Demographic Characteristics for People Under Age 65, 2001

	Population (in millions)	Type of insurance[a]			
		Employment based[b]	Public[c]	Other[d]	Uninsured
Race/ethnicity					
White	166.9	75.6%	9.3%	10.3%	11.6%
Black	31.9	56.5	23.9	7.1	20.1
Hispanic	35.5	44.8	19.4	5.1	34.7
Other	14.0	62.1	13.0	10.8	20.5
Family type					
Female-headed with children	29.6	45.3	36.3	4.8	20.5
Two parent or male-headed w/children	119.5	73.9	10.3	9.0	13.1
No children	99.2	67.6	8.9	10.7	19.4
Region					
Northeast	46.1	71.8	13.6	6.5	13.8
Midwest	55.9	74.6	11.1	8.3	12.2
South	88.5	65.0	13.3	10.2	18.8
West	57.8	63.1	13.3	10.6	19.3
Poverty level[e]					
Less than 100% of poverty	29.5	20.6	44.0	6.7	33.9
100%-149% of poverty	20.9	37.8	29.9	8.7	30.6
150%-199% of poverty	21.7	52.8	19.0	9.8	25.8
200%+ of poverty	175.6	81.5	4.7	9.6	10.7
Citizenship					
Native	219.2	70.2	13.3	9.5	13.8
Naturalized	9.6	65.8	8.8	9.7	21.0
Non-Citizens	19.5	43.5	9.7	5.7	44.3
Total	**248.3**	68.0%	12.8%	9.2%	16.5%

Source: CRS analysis of data from the March 2002 CPS.

[a] People may have more than one source of coverage; percentages may total to more than 100. [b] Group health insurance through employer or union. [c] Includes Medicare, Medicaid, the State Children's Health Insurance Program (SCHIP), and other state programs for low-income individuals. Excludes military and veterans coverage. [d] Private nongroup health insurance, veterans coverage, or military health care. [e] In 2001, the weighted average poverty threshold for a family of four was $18,104. Approximately 607,000 children are excluded from CPS-based poverty analyses because they are in unrelated subfamilies.

Employment Characteristics

Following 2 years of significant increases in employment-based coverage, the prevalence of job-related health insurance fell in 2001 to 68%. **Table 3** shows the rate of health insurance coverage by employment characteristics for people under age 65 who were workers or their dependents. In 2001, only about 8% of workers and dependents of workers in large firms (1,000 or more employees) were uninsured compared to 33% in small firms (less than 10 employees). People who reported working in small firms and their dependents accounted for 14% of the under 65 population but 28% of the uninsured. Insurance coverage varied according to industry, as well. Agriculture and personal services had the highest proportion of uninsured workers and dependents — more than 30%; only 3% of those in public administration were uninsured. Among workers, 84% of those employed full time, full year had health insurance, most often through their own employment (78%). In 2001, nearly one-third of workers with less than full time, full year employment were uninsured.

Characteristics of the Uninsured Population under Age 65

People who lack health insurance differ from the population as a whole: they are more likely to be young adults, poor, Hispanic, or employees in small firms. **Figure 1** illustrates selected characteristics of those under age 65 who were uninsured for 2001. Approximately 17% of the uninsured were 19 to 24 years old, even though this age group represents less than 9% of the under 65 population.

Our report for the year 2000 noted that for the first time since 1994, when CRS began this annual analysis, the percentage of the uninsured who were white fell below 50% — to 49%. In 2001, this percentage dropped again, to 47%, even though whites make up two-thirds (67%) of the under 65 population.

More than half (55%) of the uninsured were full time, full year workers or their dependents. Approximately 18% had no attachment to the labor force. Approximately three-quarters of the uninsured were above the poverty level. Even though the poor accounted for only 12% of the under 65 population, they represented 25% of the uninsured. For the first time since 1994, more than one-quarter of the uninsured were not native-born citizens (i.e., they were either not citizens or were naturalized citizens).

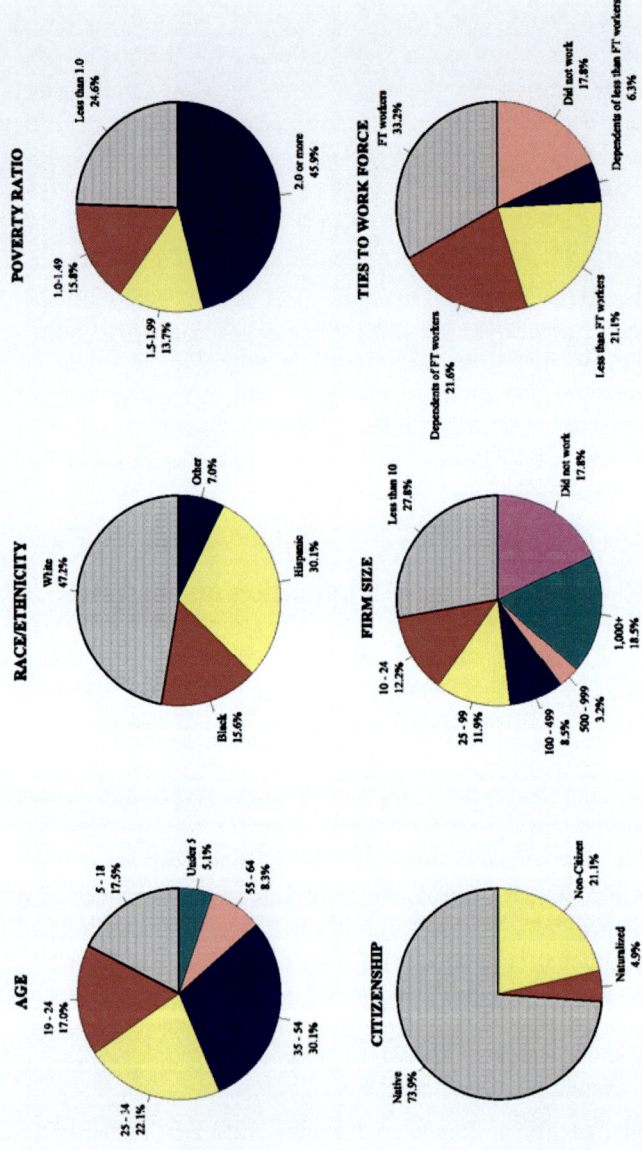

Source: Congressional Research Service (CRS) analysis of data from the March 2002 Current Population Survey (CPS)
Note: Totals may not sum to 10% due ro rounding. "FT workers" represent full-time, full-year workers.

Figure 1. Characteristics of the Uninsured Population Under Age 65, 2001

Table 3. Health Insurance Coverage by Employment Characteristics[a] for People Under Age 65, 2001

	Population (in millions)	From own job[c]	Type of insurance[b] From other's job[c]	Other[d]	Uninsured
Firm size[e]					
Under 10	34.2	20.5%	21.5%	30.5%	33.3%
10-24	18.3	31.0	28.1	20.3	27.3
25-99	27.0	37.9	36.2	16.4	18.0
100-499	30.0	40.8	42.9	14.0	11.6
500-999	12.8	42.9	43.2	12.4	10.2
1,000 +	92.2	42.5	45.5	14.4	8.2
Industry[e]					
Agriculture	4.7	16.9%	18.3%	32.0%	38.3%
Personal services	5.5	25.8	20.8	25.7	33.6
Construction	17.0	26.6	31.4	18.4	29.4
Retail trade	28.6	30.7	26.6	23.1	26.4
Entertainment	3.3	36.5	27.9	21.0	22.3
Business services	14.7	32.6	32.7	21.3	21.8
Wholesale trade	8.8	38.4	44.5	12.3	12.6
Nondurable goods	14.2	39.9	44.8	12.8	11.3
Mining	1.2	35.3	45.5	17.0	11.2
Transportation	18.5	39.7	45.6	12.6	11.2
Professional services	49.6	43.3	41.1	16.4	9.9
Durable goods	22.0	41.4	46.6	11.2	9.4
Finance/insurance	13.4	42.8	43.7	13.4	8.9
Public administration	13.2	39.9	47.0	25.5	3.4
Labor force attachment of policyholder or, if no insurance, working family member[a]					
Workers					
Full time, full year	85.3	78.2	6.6	10.6	16.0
Full time, part year	15.1	56.5	5.6	18.4	30.7
Part time, full year	6.2	46.9	6.6	24.0	33.3
Part time, part year	5.1	33.1	5.2	32.9	38.3
Workers' Dependents					
Full time, full year	84.8	0.0	77.5	18.2	10.4
Full time, part year	11.0	0.0	57.4	38.2	13.7
Part time, full year	4.3	0.0	53.1	35.4	16.5
Part time, part year	2.8	0.0	40.6	54.4	12.2

Table 3. Continued

	Population (in millions)	Type of insurance[b]			
		From own job[c]	From other's job[c]	Other[d]	Uninsured
Not working	26.3	*15.2[f]*	9.8	54.3	27.7
Coverage outside home	7.4	8.0	100.0	16.5	0.0
Total	**248.3**	34.0%	37.3%	21.4%	16.5%

Source: CRS analysis of data from the March 2002 CPS.

[a] The employment characteristics are those of the policyholder. In families without private coverage, "workers" are the family head or, if the head is not employed, the spouse. For "dependents," the employment characteristics are those of the person providing dependent coverage or, if the dependent has no private health insurance, to the head of household or spouse. [b] People may have more than one source of health insurance during the year. [c] Group health insurance through current or former employer or union. [d] Medicare, Medicaid, the State Children's Health Insurance Program (SCHIP), nongroup health insurance, veterans coverage, and other government coverage. [e] For persons who worked and their dependents. [f] Nearly 90% of these policyholders (i.e., those who did not work during the year but had employment-based coverage in their name) were retirees, were ill or disabled, or were at home with the family and probably received coverage through their former employer.

REFERENCES

[1] Includes Medicare, Medicaid, the State Children's Health Insurance Program (SCHIP), or some other program for low-income individuals. Excludes military and veterans coverage.

INDEX

A

access, viii, x, 11, 13, 15, 16, 17, 18, 19, 20, 26, 30, 34, 63, 78, 82, 84, 85, 87, 88, 89, 90, 92, 94, 95, 96, 97
accounting, 6, 15
accuracy, 18
addiction, 63
adjustment, 22, 24, 28, 30, 31, 34, 36, 42
administrators, 83
adults, 87, 93, 104, 107
advertising, 64
affect, 24, 48, 49
age, 41, 82, 92, 93, 95, 98, 100, 104, 105, 107
Age Discrimination in Employment Act, 40
alternative, 14, 15, 19, 22, 97
alternatives, 98
ambiguity, 86
amendments, 50
Americans with Disabilities Act, 85
annual rate, 2
antitrust, 58, 59, 60, 61
association, x, 78, 82, 88, 91
assumptions, 19
asymmetry, 81
attachment, 107, 109
Attorney General, 61, 70
authority, xi, 20, 33, 34, 49, 64, 65, 66, 70, 78, 93, 96
availability, 19, 86, 92
averaging, 6
awareness, 90

B

backlash, 97
baggage, 53
bargaining, 56
barriers, 64, 74, 87
base rate, 34
behavior, 58, 60, 61
benchmarks, viii, 12, 13
birds, vii
blood, 36, 39
body, 74
breakdown, 104
budget resolution, viii, 12, 13

C

Canada, ix, 45, 47, 50, 54, 55, 57, 58, 60, 61, 67, 71
carrier, 82, 83, 90
Census, xi, 5, 100, 101, 103
children, xi, 83, 87, 93, 100, 103, 105, 106

citizenship, 105
classes, 17, 20
classification, 17
closure, 51
cocaine, 63
commitment, 59
common law, 70
communication, 62
community, 17, 34
compensation, 85
competition, 30, 48, 97
complexity, 96
compliance, 51, 69
composition, 81
conduct, 14, 38, 59, 60, 66, 72, 74, 82, 83, 94
confidentiality, 18
Congressional Budget Office, viii, 12, 13
consciousness, 99
conspiracy, 59, 60, 72
consumer price index, 23, 36, 37
consumers, ix, 36, 37, 45, 46, 47, 48, 50, 51, 53, 54, 55, 56, 57, 58, 61, 62, 64, 65, 66, 67, 79, 80, 81, 86, 87, 90, 98, 99
consumption, 10
context, 80
continuity, 90
control, 17, 37, 50, 64, 97, 98, 99
Controlled Substances Act, 49, 62, 68, 73
conviction, 52
cost saving, 62
costs, vii, ix, 1, 2, 8, 14, 15, 16, 21, 23, 24, 25, 27, 29, 31, 32, 34, 36, 41, 45, 47, 48, 50, 61, 70, 80, 81, 82, 83, 87, 90, 96, 97, 98, 99
couples, 39
coverage, x, xi, 14, 15, 16, 18, 19, 21, 22, 23, 24, 25, 26, 27, 28, 31, 38, 39, 41, 67, 77, 78, 79, 80, 81, 82, 83, 84, 85, 86, 87, 88, 89, 90, 91, 92, 93, 94, 95, 96, 98, 99, 103, 104, 105, 106, 107, 110

covering, 14, 62, 83, 86, 92, 99
credit, 64
crime, 52
customers, 63
Customs and Border Protection, ix, 46, 48

D

death, 63, 82
decisions, 17, 59, 60, 99
defendants, 72
deficiency, 39
definition, 15, 63, 64, 65, 66
delivery, x, 18, 78, 96, 97
demand, 48, 79, 81, 88, 89, 90
demographic characteristics, 105
demographics, 82
denial, 33
Department of Agriculture, 73
Department of Health and Human Services, 32
Department of Justice, 57
detection, 39
diabetes, 39
dialysis, 36
disaster, x, 77, 79
discharges, 35
discipline, 65
disclosure, 85
discrimination, 86
disposable income, 81
disseminate, 14
distribution, 48, 49, 53, 62, 63, 80, 83, 89
diversity, 92
doctors, ix, 46, 49, 62, 63, 64, 65, 66, 75
dominance, 95
dosage, 54
drugs, vii, ix, 2, 3, 6, 9, 15, 16, 17, 18, 20, 21, 23, 26, 27, 32, 35, 36, 38, 41, 45, 46, 47, 48, 49, 50, 51, 52, 53, 54, 55, 56, 57, 58, 61, 62, 63, 64, 65, 66, 67, 68, 70, 71, 74

E

earnings, 42, 92
economic resources, 5
economies of scale, 90
elderly, 92, 93, 94
election, 27, 30
email, 62
employees, vii, x, 26, 27, 40, 42, 55, 78, 79, 83, 84, 86, 88, 107
employment, x, xi, 77, 79, 82, 84, 88, 89, 90, 95, 98, 103, 104, 105, 107, 110
end-stage renal disease, 33
energy, 99
enrollment, 14, 15, 19, 20, 22, 23, 25, 26, 27, 30, 84, 89, 92
environment, 86
equipment, 9, 36, 37
equity, viii, 12, 13
ESI, 84, 88, 89, 90, 94
estimating, 81
ethnicity, 106
evidence, 17, 53, 59, 60, 61, 72
exclusion, 41, 84, 91
exercise, 55, 64, 74
expectation, 99
expenditures, vii, 1, 2, 3, 5, 6, 8, 15, 23, 31, 32, 80, 91
experts, 4, 10

F

family, xi, 16, 41, 80, 81, 83, 100, 101, 103, 105, 106, 109, 110
family members, xi, 103
fasting, 39
FDA, ix, 45, 46, 47, 48, 49, 50, 51, 52, 53, 54, 55, 56, 57, 58, 61, 62, 63, 67, 68, 69, 70, 71, 72, 73, 74
FDA approval, 51
federal courts, 52
federal funds, 8
federal law, 55, 56, 59, 61, 62, 63, 85

finance, 81
financial resources, 95
financing, vii, 2, 31, 42, 96, 97
firms, 84, 86, 90, 91, 107
flexibility, 81
foreign language, 52
fraud, 2, 17, 53
fulfillment, 72
funding, viii, 12, 13, 31, 32, 33, 41, 99

G

GDP, vii, 1, 5, 6
General Motors, 72
glucose, 39
God, 101
goods and services, vii, 1, 2, 3, 5, 10
government, x, 2, 8, 21, 42, 63, 67, 77, 79, 87, 110
grants, 61, 87
gross domestic product, vii, 1
group size, 91
groups, 22, 23, 41, 79, 80, 82, 83, 90, 91, 94, 99, 104
growth, x, 2, 4, 5, 28, 31, 77, 79, 84, 89, 97
growth rate, 2, 5
guidance, 32, 54
guidelines, 18, 20, 66, 75, 93

H

harm, 58
Hawaii, 40
health, vii, viii, x, xi, 1, 2, 3, 5, 6, 7, 8, 9, 10, 12, 13, 17, 21, 24, 26, 27, 32, 35, 37, 38, 41, 49, 50, 51, 53, 54, 65, 77, 78, 79, 80, 81, 82, 83, 84, 85, 86, 87, 88, 89, 90, 91, 92, 93, 94, 95, 96, 97, 98, 99, 103, 104, 105, 106, 107, 110
health care, vii, viii, x, 1, 2, 3, 5, 6, 8, 9, 10, 12, 13, 17, 38, 41, 65, 77, 78, 79,

80, 81, 85, 86, 87, 90, 92, 93, 94, 95, 96, 97, 98, 99
health care costs, 86, 97, 98
health expenditure, vii, 1, 2, 3, 4, 5, 32, 80
health information, 86
health insurance, vii, x, xi, 2, 3, 8, 9, 21, 41, 77, 78, 79, 80, 81, 82, 83, 84, 85, 86, 87, 88, 89, 90, 91, 92, 93, 94, 95, 97, 99, 103, 104, 105, 106, 107, 110
health problems, 94
health services, vii, 1, 8, 10, 38, 41, 80, 81, 87, 89, 96, 98, 99
health status, 24, 81, 86, 89
heroin, 63
higher quality, 4
Hispanics, 105
hospice, 92
House, viii, ix, 11, 12, 32, 41, 45, 47, 73

I

implementation, 26, 33, 50, 51, 54, 97
imports, ix, 46, 48, 49, 50, 51, 53, 55, 56, 67
imprisonment, 52
incentives, viii, 12, 29, 97, 98, 99
income, viii, 12, 13, 14, 16, 22, 23, 26, 27, 39, 41, 42, 79, 84, 86, 87, 89, 93, 95, 99, 101, 104, 106, 110
income tax, 42, 86
indication, 6
indicators, 35
indices, 4
industrialized countries, 84
industry, 56, 65, 82, 97, 107
inflation, 2, 97
influence, 98
infrastructure, 41
initiation, 74
inmates, 55
institutions, 7, 97
insurance, viii, x, xi, 2, 8, 9, 10, 16, 41, 67, 77, 78, 79, 80, 81, 82, 83, 84, 85, 86, 87, 88, 89, 90, 91, 93, 94, 95, 96, 97, 98, 99, 103, 104, 105, 106, 107, 109, 110
intensity, 4
intent, 52
interest, vii, ix, xi, 35, 42, 43, 45, 47, 64, 66, 67, 78, 85, 88, 97, 98
interest groups, 66, 67
Internal Revenue Service, x, 77, 79, 84
international trade, 57, 71
interpersonal interactions, 66
intervention, 38
investment, 35, 47, 98
invitation to participate, 60

J

jobs, 86, 90, 94
judges, 70
jurisdiction, 64, 73, 74
justification, 50

K

knowledge, x, 3, 77, 79

L

labeling, 49, 51, 56, 70
labor, 34, 95, 107
labor force, 95, 107
land, vii, 70
language, 70
laws, vii, 48, 49, 58, 59, 60, 61, 62, 63, 65, 66, 70, 74, 85
lead, x, 63, 78, 99
leadership, 47
legislation, viii, x, 12, 13, 14, 15, 31, 32, 36, 50, 54, 56, 64, 68, 77, 79, 88, 96, 97
liability, 61, 69
likelihood, 57, 80, 88
litigation, 86

Index

local government, 55, 56
location, 51, 83
lower prices, ix, 16, 46, 47

M

mammography, 39
management, 17, 21, 38, 80, 84, 85, 97, 98
manufacturing, 48, 49, 51, 62, 63
market, 36, 37, 52, 61, 81, 82, 83, 84, 89, 91, 93, 94, 97
market share, 81, 97
marketing, 21, 84
markets, 49, 51, 61
measures, ix, 4, 12, 13, 17, 32
Medicaid, viii, xi, 3, 4, 5, 6, 7, 8, 9, 12, 15, 22, 23, 26, 32, 37, 40, 43, 55, 89, 93, 100, 103, 104, 106, 110
Medicare, v, viii, ix, 3, 4, 5, 6, 7, 8, 9, 11, 12, 13, 14, 15, 22, 23, 25, 26, 27, 28, 29, 30, 31, 32, 33, 34, 35, 36, 37, 38, 39, 40, 41, 42, 43, 45, 47, 50, 54, 67, 68, 69, 89, 92, 93, 94, 95, 104, 106, 110
medication, 17, 18, 65, 75
methodology, 36
military, 26, 106, 110
minority, x, 78, 80, 88, 92
models, 97
modernization, viii, 11, 12, 13
money, 33, 55, 98, 104
monitoring, 52
moratorium, 37
motion, 60, 61
motivation, 86

N

narcotics, 49, 63
negative consequences, 87
negotiating, 67, 91
negotiation, 20

network, 16, 27, 29, 97
non-citizens, 105
nursing, vii, 1, 2, 6, 35, 92, 93

O

obligation, 65
opiates, 49, 63
organization, 15, 16, 19, 22, 23, 28, 29, 30, 65, 66, 74, 82, 83
organizations, 18, 19, 24, 30, 65, 83, 97, 98
oxygen, 37

P

pain, 63
parents, 87, 93, 104, 105
penalties, 22, 49, 52, 53
pensions, 85
per capita income, 48
permit, 16, 17, 53, 54
persons with disabilities, 92, 93
perspective, 2, 90
plants, 47
plasma, 39
pools, 81, 88, 89, 90, 94, 101
poor, x, 78, 87, 95, 105, 107
population, 3, 5, 80, 81, 88, 89, 92, 93, 94, 95, 99, 104, 105, 107
population growth, 3
portability, 86, 90
ports, 67
poverty, 14, 22, 23, 27, 93, 101, 105, 106, 107
power, 56
preference, 84
pregnancy, 89
premiums, 8, 9, 21, 23, 24, 25, 30, 31, 39, 42, 81, 86, 94, 97
price index, 4
prices, ix, x, 3, 4, 14, 15, 16, 18, 26, 41, 45, 47, 48, 58, 60, 67, 78, 87

principle, 5
privacy, 19, 62, 86
private sector, x, 2, 78, 88
production, 61
profit margin, 61
profits, 47, 57
program, viii, ix, x, 11, 12, 13, 14, 15, 16, 17, 18, 25, 26, 27, 28, 29, 30, 31, 32, 33, 36, 37, 38, 40, 41, 42, 45, 47, 55, 64, 65, 78, 88, 92, 93, 104, 110
proliferation, 65
public administration, 107
public health, vii, 1, 2, 3, 57
public pension, 55
public sector, 2
pumps, 37

Q

quality assurance, 17, 97

R

race, 105
range, 2, 25, 53, 83, 93, 99
reality, 65
recognition, 18
reconciliation, 25
redistribution, 35
reduction, 15, 16, 20, 35, 50, 51, 54
regulation, ix, 46, 48, 62, 65, 84, 85
regulations, 32, 37, 62, 83, 85
regulators, ix, 46, 48, 61
rehabilitation, 34
reinsurance, 19, 22, 24
relationship, 66, 91
relationships, 87
relative size, 6
resolution, 13
resources, 22, 23, 53
responsibility, 48, 49, 53, 65, 85, 99
retail, 7
retention, 88

retirement, 42
returns, 39
revenue, viii, 12, 13, 31, 32, 41, 42, 43, 97
rights, 85
risk, 14, 19, 20, 21, 22, 24, 25, 28, 29, 37, 38, 39, 47, 49, 50, 51, 53, 54, 55, 80, 81, 82, 83, 88, 89, 90, 91, 94, 95, 101
risk profile, 19

S

safety, ix, 17, 41, 46, 47, 48, 49, 50, 52, 54, 55, 57, 58, 61, 62, 65, 67
sales, ix, 36, 46, 48, 57, 58, 59, 60, 61, 62, 64, 67, 84, 90
sanctions, 49, 62, 63
satisfaction, 30, 38
savings, viii, 12, 25, 28, 29, 30, 31, 41, 42, 86, 98
savings account, viii, 12, 41, 86, 98
scarcity, 34
search, 64, 67, 98
security, 41, 100
self, 41, 42, 81, 83, 84, 85, 86, 91, 94
self-employed, 42, 86, 94
Senate, viii, ix, 11, 12, 13, 32, 45, 47
services, vii, x, 1, 3, 6, 27, 28, 29, 33, 34, 35, 36, 37, 38, 62, 77, 78, 79, 80, 81, 83, 84, 85, 86, 87, 89, 90, 92, 93, 94, 96, 99, 107, 109
shares, 88
sharing, 15, 16, 17, 18, 22, 23, 25, 38, 39, 83, 90, 97
Sherman Act, 59, 60, 72
sign, 84
sites, 30, 38, 62, 63, 64, 65, 66
small firms, 84, 91, 107
social security, 22
solvency, 21
spectrum, 91, 98
stabilization, viii, 12, 13, 29, 42
standard of living, 3, 10

standardization, 60
standards, 17, 18, 21, 65, 66, 74, 85
state regulators, 64
statutes, 59, 61
storage, 58
strategies, 80, 88, 89, 90
strength, 17, 66
subsidy, 16, 19, 21, 22, 23, 24, 25, 31, 41
summer, 55
supervision, 48, 62
suppliers, 9
supply, 17, 53, 54, 58, 61, 68
Supreme Court, 59, 60
surplus, 60
surprise, 96
survival, 4
survival rate, 4
systems, x, 33, 78, 96

T

tactics, 59
targets, 38
taxation, x, 31, 77
teaching, 35
technology, 3, 18, 62, 66
tension, 58
therapy, 17, 37, 92
threshold, 16, 23, 24, 25, 36, 106
time, viii, x, xi, 4, 7, 11, 13, 17, 18, 19, 21, 26, 31, 34, 35, 55, 60, 77, 79, 81, 86, 89, 90, 94, 95, 96, 99, 103, 107, 108, 109
time frame, 89
trade, x, 59, 78, 82, 88, 90, 91, 109
trade union, 82
transmission, 86

trend, xi, 5, 7, 103
trial, 72
trust, 31, 32, 42, 43, 59

U

uncertainty, 80, 81
uniform, 21, 22, 60, 63, 65
unions, 88
United States, ix, xi, 17, 20, 45, 47, 49, 50, 52, 54, 56, 57, 58, 59, 60, 61, 69, 70, 71, 72, 84, 100, 103
updating, 28
urban areas, 34

V

values, 34, 35
variables, 96

W

wages, 10, 84, 86, 90, 98
web, 55
welfare, 85
wholesale, 36
women, 93
words, 81, 85
work, 41, 66, 79, 84, 88, 95, 98, 104, 110
workers, xi, 10, 42, 78, 79, 84, 88, 90, 94, 95, 97, 98, 103, 104, 107, 108, 110
workplace, x, 77, 84, 89, 93, 94, 95, 98
World War I, 88
writing, 53, 92